USB Embedded Hosts

The Developer's Guide

Jan Axelson

Lakeview Research LLC
Madison, WI 53704

USB Embedded Hosts
by Jan Axelson
Copyright 2011, 2016 by Janet L. Axelson

The source code in this book is available for downloading at janaxelson.com

Published by **Lakeview Research LLC**
janaxelson.com
Distributed by **Independent Publishers Group**
ipgbook.com

14 13 12 11 10 9 8 7 6 5 4 3 2

Printed and bound in the United States of America
ISBN13 978-1-931448-24-6

Contents

Introduction

USB isn't just for mainstream PCs anymore. With hardware and firmware support, small embedded systems can use the same devices available to conventional desktop and notebook PCs.

Data loggers can store data on USB drives. Robotic arms can receive input from USB keyboards. Sales terminals can print receipts on USB printers. USB cameras, speakers, mics, network bridges, virtual serial ports, Bluetooth adapters, and more can be available to the embedded systems you create. This book will show you how.

What's Inside

If you are interested in designing, programming, or learning about small systems that access USB devices, this book is for you.

The first two chapters are an introduction to the USB interface and USB hosts in embedded systems.

Chapter 1, *USB Essentials,* is a whirlwind tour of what you need to know about USB hardware and protocols to develop a USB embedded host system.

Chapter 2, *USB Hosts for Embedded Systems*, explains how USB embedded hosts differ from USB hosts in conventional PCs. You'll learn which USB host requirements are relaxed for embedded systems and what new requirements some USB embedded host systems must meet. A guide to USB embedded host hardware and software will help you select a development platform that matches your project's needs.

Many USB embedded host systems use the Linux operating system because of its rich support for USB host communications. The next two chapters focus on tools and techniques for developing USB embedded host systems that use Linux.

Chapter 3, *Using Linux in Embedded Systems*, presents options for using Linux in small systems and introduces the BeagleBoard-xM open development platform. You'll learn how to manage permissions on an embedded Linux system, how to run an application at startup, and how the applications you write can provide debugging data.

Chapter 4, *Exploring USB in Linux*, shows how to use Linux commands and utilities to learn about, monitor, and debug communications with attached USB devices.

The heart of the book focuses on communicating with USB devices. The chapters that follow discuss USB communications for a variety of USB peripheral types with example code for Linux USB host systems.

Chapter 5, *Accessing Files on Drives*, shows how to detect attached USB drives and how to read and write to files on USB drives.

Chapter 6, *Getting User Input*, introduces the USB human interface device class and shows how to read user input from USB keyboards.

Chapter 7, *Bridging to Other Interfaces*, shows how USB can function as a bridge to other interfaces such as serial ports, wired and wireless networks, and Bluetooth.

Chapter 8, *Printing*, introduces printer-control languages and shows how applications can print documents on USB printers.

Chapter 9, *Using Sound and Video*, shows how to use USB mics, speakers, and cameras to record and play audio and video streams.

Chapter 10, *Communicating with Vendor-defined Devices*, shows how to communicate with devices that don't fit standard USB classes, including devices that transfer vendor-defined data, HID-class devices that perform vendor-defined functions, and a display monitor that uses a USB interface and vendor-specific driver.

Chapter 11, *Implementing a Dual-role Port*, shows how a USB On-The-Go (OTG) port can function as both a host and device port. An example application configures an OTG system to function as a USB drive when attached to a USB host.

To get the most from this book, some experience with the USB interface is helpful. Whatever development platform you use, you'll need to be familiar with how to compile, load, and run applications on your embedded system.

About the Example Code

Embedded-system developers have many choices for hardware and software platforms. For this book's example code, I chose the BeagleBoard-xM open development board (*beagleboard.org*) with an Ubuntu Netbook distribution of Linux for ARM (*elinux.org/BeagleBoardUbuntu*). The example code is largely portable to other Linux systems, and the concepts behind the code apply to systems that use other development platforms.

Updates and More

To find out more about developing USB embedded host systems, I invite you to visit my website at *janaxelson.com*. You'll find the program code from the book along with links to products, tools, and information related to developing for USB.

My website will also have any corrections and updates to the book. If you find an error, please let me know.

Text Conventions

This book uses these formatting conventions:

Complete commands to be typed are in **`bold monospace`**.

User options in commands are in ***`bold italic monospace`***.

Source code, system responses to commands, and file and program names are in `regular monospace`.

URLs and titles are in *italics*.

Acknowledgements

This book wouldn't exist without the advice, encouragement, and other help from many people.

Thanks to hardware expert, Linux advocate, and talented technical writer Ed Nisley for reviewing my Linux code and text.

Thanks to Xiaofan Chen for his excellent libusb code, which I used as a model for my libusb examples.

Thanks to Gus Issa at GHI Electronics for providing samples of USB host products and for interesting discussions about embedded systems.

Thanks to Dave Riness and the others at FTDI for providing Vinculum II samples.

Thanks to Gerald Coley and Jason Kridner for their hard work and dedication in developing and promoting the popular BeagleBoard development system. Thanks also to everyone who generously shared their knowledge and experience in the Beagle-Board discussion group (*beagleboard.org/discuss*).

With that said, any and all errors in this book are mine and mine alone.

I hope you find this book useful and welcome your comments at *jan@janaxelson.com*.

1

USB Essentials

This chapter is a quick tour of the minimum you need to know about USB hardware and protocols when developing USB embedded host systems.

How Data Travels on the Bus

USB is a universal serial bus developed to handle communications between personal computers (PCs) and peripherals that have varying needs. Every USB communication is between a USB host and a USB device. The host can be a PC or an embedded system with USB host capability. The USB host manages traffic on the bus. Devices respond to communications from the host.

The USB Implementers Forum (USB-IF at *usb.org*) is the trade group that publishes the *Universal Serial Bus Specification* and other documents that are the ultimate reference to the interface. The USB-IF also sponsors conferences and provides tools, compliance tests, and other resources for developers.

A companion to the USB specifications is my book *USB Complete*, a developer's guide to the interface and designing and programming USB peripherals.

Bus Speeds

At this writing, most USB devices use the USB 2.0 interface, which has a 2-wire data bus and supports three signaling rates: high speed at 480 Mbps, full speed at 12 Mbps, and low speed at 1.5 Mbps. Data travels on the data wires (D+ and D-) in one direction at a time. USB 3.0 added SuperSpeed, which uses a 4-wire bus and has a signaling rate of 5 Gbps. With SuperSpeed, each direction has its own pair of wires, and data can travel in both directions at the same time.

In addition to the signaling rate, factors that affect throughput on the bus are the type of transfer, the capabilities and performance of the host and device hardware, the efficiency of the program code in the host and device, and how busy the bus is.

All USB cables have power (VBUS) and ground wires that provide a nominal +5V supply to the downstream device.

Devices

Every USB device has one or more endpoints, which are buffers that store received data or data ready to transmit. Each endpoint address has an assigned number, direction, transfer type, and maximum number of data bytes the endpoint can send or receive in a transaction.

A hub is a special type of device with one port that connects to the host or another upstream hub and one or more downstream ports that can connect to devices, which may include other hubs. Hubs, including the root hub in the host, provide power to their downstream devices. Some devices provide their own power to supplement the bus power.

Transfers

A USB transfer consists of one or more transactions that can carry data to or from an endpoint. Table 1-1 shows the phases that make up a USB 2.0 transaction.

Phase	Purpose
Token	The host specifies a device, endpoint number, and direction for the data phase.
Data	The host sends data to the device or the device sends data to the host.
Handshake	The recipient of data in the data phase sends information about the success or failure of the transaction.

Table 1-1: Each transaction contains token and data phases, and most transactions have a handshake phase.

In the token phase, the host initiates a transaction by sending a token packet that specifies the device, endpoint number, and direction of the data phase. An IN token packet requests a data packet from the endpoint. A SETUP or OUT token packet precedes a data packet from the host.

In the data phase, the host or device sends data depending on the direction specified in the token phase. In addition to data, each data packet contains error-checking bits and a packet ID (PID) with a data-sequencing value that helps the receiver of the data detect missing packets.

In the handshake phase, the receiver of data in the data phase reports the success or failure of the transaction. Some transactions have fixed scheduling that doesn't allow retrying after an error, and these transactions don't have a handshake phase.

On a SuperSpeed bus, transactions perform similar functions, but the protocol differs due to the 4-wire bus and the need to support SuperSpeed's added capabilities for power saving and other features.

Transfer Types

USB supports four transfer types: control, bulk, interrupt, and isochronous. As Table 1-2 shows, each type has capabilities suited for a particular set of needs.

Transfer Type	Control	Bulk	Interrupt	Isochronous
Device support required?	yes	no	no	no
Low speed allowed?	yes	no	yes	no
Error correction provided?	yes	yes	yes	no
Guaranteed transfer rate?	no	no	no	yes
Guaranteed maximum latency?	no	no	yes	yes
Typical use	enumeration	printer	keyboard	audio

Table 1-2: USB has four transfer types to support the needs of different peripheral types.

Control transfers send requests and receive responses where the timing isn't critical. The host reserves a portion of the bus bandwidth for control transfers, but an individual transfer has to share the bus with other devices and has no guaranteed timing.

On device attachment or bootup with a device attached, the host uses control transfers to request data structures called descriptors from the device. The descriptors provide information about the device's capabilities and help the host decide what driver to assign to the device. The process of retrieving descriptors and assigning a driver is called enumeration. A device-class specification can also define class-specific control requests.

Each control transfer has two or three stages: Setup, Data (optional), and Status. In the Setup stage, the host sends a request to the device. The Data stage, if present, carries data from the host or device, depending on the request. The Status stage carries information about the success of the transfer.

In the Setup stage, the host provides information in these fields:

bmRequestType is a bit field that specifies the direction of data flow, the request type, and the recipient.

Bit 7 names the direction of data flow for data in the Data stage. Host to device (OUT) or no Data stage is zero; device to host (IN) is 1.

Bits 6..5 specify whether the request is one of USB's standard requests (00), a request defined for a specific USB class (01), or a request defined by a vendor-specific driver for use with a particular product or products (10).

Bits 4..0 specify whether the request is directed to the device (00000) or to an interface (00001), endpoint (00010), or other element (00011) in the device.

bRequest is the request number defined by the host's driver.

wValue is defined by the request. For example, in the HID-class Get_Report request, wValue contains the report type and report ID.

wIndex is defined by the request. A typical use is to pass an index or offset such as an interface or endpoint number.

wLength is the number of bytes the host will transfer in the Data stage or the maximum number of bytes the device should return in the Data stage. If zero, the transfer has no Data stage.

The other transfer types don't have defined stages. Instead, higher-level software defines how to use the data being transferred.

Bulk transfers are the fastest on an otherwise idle bus but have no guaranteed timing. Printers, drives, and network communications use bulk transfers.

Interrupt transfers have guaranteed maximum latency, or time between transaction attempts. For example, with a maximum latency of 10 ms, the host can schedule a transaction every 10 ms or more frequently. Interrupt transactions are suited for devices that need to send or receive data without delay. Mice and keyboards use interrupt transfers to send data about key presses and mouse movements.

Isochronous transfers have guaranteed timing but no error correcting. Streaming audio and video, which needs precise timing and can tolerate occasional errors, uses isochronous transfers.

Endpoint zero supports control transfers. The other transfer types can use any other available endpoint address on the device hardware. Low-speed devices can use only control and interrupt transfers. Full-speed, high-speed, and SuperSpeed devices can use all four transfer types.

How the Host Communicates with Devices

To communicate with an attached device, a USB host must use class or vendor-defined protocols supported by the device. The data may also use industry protocols to implement higher-level functions. For example, to read and write to drives, the USB host uses bulk transfers to send SCSI commands to the device. To play audio, a USB host can use isochronous transfers to send an MP3 file to USB speakers. A host platform that has built-in support for the needed protocols can give a big head start to a project.

Device Classes

The USB-IF publishes class specifications for common device functions (Table 1-3). Each class has a code that devices can declare in a descriptor. Devices with vendor-specific drivers use the class code FFh, and the host identifies the specific device by the Vendor ID and Product ID in the device descriptor. Hosts may also use the Vendor ID and Product ID to identify specific devices in a standard class. For example, the host may want to identify a HID-class device that performs a particular vendor-defined function.

In conventional PCs, the operating system (OS) provides drivers for accessing devices in popular classes. In embedded-host platforms, the built-in support may be limited to a couple of popular device types such as flash drives and keyboards. Or a platform may provide partial support, such as the ability to send data to USB printers, but leave it to the developer to support printer languages or specific printer features.

A device that doesn't belong to a defined class can use a custom driver tailored to the device's function or a driver that can exchange generic data with the device. Some embedded-host platforms support popular devices with vendor-defined functions. An example is the FT232x USB UART chips from Future Technology Devices International (FTDI). The chips have support in FTDI's Vinculum II USB host module and in distributions of Linux for embedded systems.

Chapter 1

USB Class	Class Code (hexadecimal)	Descriptor that Declares the Class
Audio (speakers, mics, MIDI)	01	Interface
Communications devices (CDC) (virtual COM port, Ethernet bridge, wireless mobile handset)	02	Device and interface or interface
Content security	0D	Interface
Device firmware upgrade (DFU)	FE subclass 01	Interface and subclass
Hub	09	Device
Human interface device (HID) (keyboard, mouse, game controller, vendor-specific function)	03	Interface
Imaging (scanners)	06	Interface
IrDA bridge	FE subclass 02	Interface and subclass
Mass storage (drive)	08	Interface
Personal healthcare	0F	Device or interface
Printer	07	Interface
Smart card	0B	Interface
Test and measurement	FE subclass 03	Interface and subclass
Vendor-defined	FF	Device or interface
Video	0E	Interface
Wireless controller (Bluetooth bridge)	E0	Device or interface

Table 1-3: The USB-IF defines classes for popular peripheral functions.

Learning about Attached Devices

A host learns about a device by examining the descriptors retrieved during enumeration. Listing 1-1 shows descriptors for a device that uses a vendor-specific driver.

```
Device Descriptor
12        bLength              Descriptor size in bytes
01        bDescriptorType      Descriptor type (device)
0200      bcdUSB               USB Specification release number (BCD)
                               (2.00)
00        bDeviceClass         Class Code (class defined in interface
                               descriptor)
00        bDeviceSubClass      Subclass code
00        bDeviceProtocol      Protocol code
08        bMaxPacketSize0      Endpoint 0 maximum packet size
0925      idVendor             Vendor ID (assigned by USB-IF)
1456      idProduct            Product ID (assigned by vendor)
0100      bcdDevice            Device release number (BCD)
00        iManufacturer        Manufacturer string index
00        iProduct             Product string index
00        iSerialNumber        Device serial number string index
01        bNumConfigurations   Number of configurations

Configuration Descriptor
09        bLength              Descriptor size in bytes
02        bDescriptorType      Descriptor type (configuration)
002E      wTotalLength         Total length of this and subordinate
                               descriptors
01        bNumInterfaces       Number of interfaces in this configuration
01        bConfigurationValue  Index of this configuration
00        iConfiguration       Configuration string index
E0        bmAttributes         Attributes (self powered, remote wakeup
                               supported)
32        bMaxPower            1/2 maximum bus current requested (100 mA)
```

Listing 1-1: These descriptors are for a device that uses a vendor-specific driver. Descriptor values are in hexadecimal. (Part 1 of 3)

```
Interface Descriptor
09       bLength             Descriptor size in bytes
04       bDescriptorType     Descriptor type (interface)
00       bInterfaceNumber    Interface number
00       bAlternateSetting   Alternate setting number
04       bNumEndpoints       Number of endpoints in this interface
FF       bInterfaceClass     Interface class (vendor specific)
00       bInterfaceSubclass  Interface subclass
00       bInterfaceProtocol  Interface protocol
00       iInterface          Interface string index

Interrupt IN Endpoint Descriptor
07       bLength             Descriptor size in bytes
05       bDescriptorType     Descriptor type (endpoint)
81       bEndpointAddress    Endpoint number and direction (1 IN)
03       bmAttributes        Transfer type (interrupt)
0008     wMaxPacketSize      Maximum packet size
0A       bInterval           Polling interval (ms)

Interrupt OUT Endpoint Descriptor
07       bLength             Descriptor size in bytes
05       bDescriptorType     Descriptor type (endpoint)
01       bEndpointAddress    Endpoint number and direction (1 OUT)
03       bmAttributes        Transfer type (interrupt)
0008     wMaxPacketSize      Maximum packet size
0A       bInterval           Polling interval (ms)

Bulk IN Endpoint Descriptor
07       bLength             Descriptor size in bytes
05       bDescriptorType     Descriptor type (endpoint)
82       bEndpointAddress    Endpoint number and direction (2 IN)
02       bmAttributes        Transfer type (bulk)
0040     wMaxPacketSize      Maximum packet size
00       bInterval           Polling interval (ignored for bulk endpoint)
```

Listing 1-1: These descriptors are for a device that uses a vendor-specific driver. Descriptor values are in hexadecimal. (Part 2 of 3)

```
Bulk OUT Endpoint Descriptor
07        bLength               Descriptor size in bytes
05        bDescriptorType       Descriptor type (endpoint)
02        bEndpointAddress      Endpoint number and direction (2 OUT)
02        bmAttributes          Transfer type (bulk)
0040      wMaxPacketSize        Maximum packet size
00        bInterval             Polling interval (ignored for bulk endpoint)
```

Listing 1-1: These descriptors are for a device that uses a vendor-specific driver. Descriptor values are in hexadecimal. (Part 3 of 3)

Every device has a device descriptor that specifies the device's Vendor ID, Product ID, device release number, maximum packet size for endpoint zero, and number of configurations. The device descriptor can also specify a class, subclass, and protocol. A function specified in the device descriptor applies to the entire device and thus limits the device to a single function. Table 1-4 shows fields that a host can examine in the device descriptor to learn a device's function.

Descriptor Field	Code (hexadecimal)	Use
bDeviceClass	00	The interface descriptor(s) specify the function and the function doesn't have an interface association descriptor.
	01-EE	USB class code.
	EF	The interface descriptor(s) specify the function and the function has an interface association descriptor.
	FF	Vendor-defined function.
bDeviceSubclass	00	Defined by the class named in bDeviceClass. Typically "No subclass."
	01-FE	Subclass defined by the class named in bDeviceClass.
	FF	Vendor-defined subclass.
bDeviceProtocol	00	Device protocols not supported.
	01-FE	Protocol defined by the class named in bDeviceClass.
	FF	Vendor-defined protocol.

Table 1-4: The device descriptor can declare a function or indicate that one or more interface descriptor(s) declare the device's function(s). (Part 1 of 2)

Descriptor Field	Code (hexadecimal)	Use
idVendor	0000-FFFF	Vendor ID assigned by the USB-IF.
idProduct	0000-FFFF	Product ID assigned by the owner of the Vendor ID.
bcdDevice	0000-FFFF	Device release number assigned by the owner of the Vendor ID.

Table 1-4: The device descriptor can declare a function or indicate that one or more interface descriptor(s) declare the device's function(s). (Part 2 of 2)

The idVendor and idProduct fields contain the Vendor ID and Product ID that identify the specific device. The bcdDevice field can further identify the device by release number.

A configuration descriptor specifies the amount of bus current the device needs with bMaxPower equal to half the requested bus current in mA. In Listing 1-1, bMaxPower = 32h, so the requested current is 32h × 2, which equals 64h or 100 mA.

Each configuration descriptor has one or more subordinate interface descriptors. If bDeviceClass in the device descriptor equals 00h or EFh, the device defines its function or functions in one or more interface descriptors. Devices declare most functions in interface descriptors. Table 1-5 shows fields in the interface descriptor that can identify an interface's class.

Descriptor Field	Code (hexadecimal)	Use
bInterfaceClass	00	Reserved.
	01-FE	USB class code.
	FF	Vendor-defined function.
bInterfaceSubclass	00	Defined by the class named in bInterfaceClass. Typically "No subclass."
	01-FE	Subclass defined by the class named in bInterfaceClass.
	FF	Vendor-defined subclass.
bInterfaceProtocol	00	Interface protocols not supported.
	01-FE	Protocol defined by the class named in bInterfaceClass.
	FF	Vendor-defined protocol.

Table 1-5: For some classes, an interface descriptor can specify a device function.

A device that specifies its function(s) in interface descriptors can have multiple functions. For example, a device can function as both a printer and a mass-storage device with each function having an interface descriptor. In Listing 1-1's example descriptor, bInterfaceClass assigns a vendor-specific function to the interface.

A class or vendor function can use subclass and protocol codes to further define a device's function and protocols. An example is devices in the application-specific class (FEh), which use the subclass field to specify the function.

Some classes, such as audio, use multiple interfaces to implement a single function. For these devices, an interface association descriptor (IAD) can indicate which interfaces belong to a function.

An interface may have zero or more subordinate endpoint descriptors. An endpoint descriptor specifies the endpoint's number and direction, transfer type, maximum packet size, and polling interval, if any. The wMaxPacketSize field specifies the maximum number of data bytes the endpoint can transfer in a transaction. To transfer more than the maximum packet size in a single transfer, the host uses multiple transactions.

Listing 1-1's descriptors have an interrupt and bulk endpoint for each direction. Endpoint zero, required for all devices, never has an endpoint descriptor, always supports control transfers, and is bidirectional. In the device descriptor, bMaxPacketSize0 specifies endpoint zero's maximum packet size.

The USB 2.0 specification and other documents from the USB-IF define additional descriptor types. A string descriptor can store text such as a manufacturer's name, product name, or serial number. A class specification can define a class-specific descriptor. For example, HID-class devices have a class-specific HID descriptor and at least one class-specific report descriptor.

You can view a device's descriptors by attaching the device to a host and viewing the traffic with a hardware protocol analyzer or a software analyzer that captures enumeration traffic. Chapter 4 shows how to use the Linux `lsusb` command to view descriptors of attached devices.

2

USB Hosts for Embedded Systems

Developers have many choices for hardware and programming for USB embedded host systems. This chapter will help you choose a platform that has the USB host capabilities your project needs.

Embedded Hosts are Different

Because embedded systems typically support a limited number of peripheral types, most USB hosts in embedded systems don't need the full capabilities of a conventional USB host. At the same time, some USB hosts in embedded systems need capabilities that conventional hosts don't have, such as the option to turn off bus power when the bus is idle.

Dedicated Functions

A conventional PC's function and attached peripherals vary with the applications that users install and run. A PC in a science lab might connect to a variety of lab instruments, while a home PC might need to support the latest game controller. USB hosts in conventional PCs must support the wide variety of devices that users might attach.

To do so, the host supports multiple bus speeds and external hubs. Each host port can provide 500 mA (900 mA for SuperSpeed) to an attached device. The operating system (OS) provides drivers for popular USB device classes, and users can load drivers for additional devices as needed.

In contrast, embedded systems have defined functions. The firmware programmed into the system determines the system's function and the number and types of supported USB devices. These devices in turn determine what speeds the host must support, whether the host needs to support external hubs, and how much current the host port(s) must provide. Adding support for new devices typically requires a firmware update.

Some embedded systems provide both USB host and USB device functions. These systems may have a dedicated port for each function or a single dual-role port that can serve as both a host and device port, swapping roles as needed.

The Targeted Peripheral List

To reduce user confusion and frustration, a USB embedded host system can provide a Targeted Peripheral List that names devices that are known to work with the system. For example, a vendor might list manufacturers and model numbers of tested printers. Other printer models may also work, but the list enables users to rely on known good peripherals.

The USB-IF's *On-The-Go and Embedded Host Supplement to the USB Revision 2.0 Specification* defines requirements for USB host systems that provide a Targeted Peripheral List. The specification calls these systems Targeted Hosts.

Two types of Targeted Hosts are Embedded Host and On-The-Go (OTG) systems (Figure 2-1).

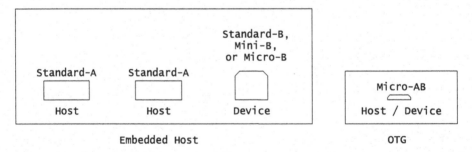

Figure 2-1. An Embedded Host system can have multiple USB ports, while an OTG system has a single dual-role port.

An Embedded Host system has one or more host ports and may also have a device port. An OTG system has a single port that can function as both a host and device port. Some requirements are relaxed for Targeted Host systems, and OTG systems have added responsibilities for managing the dual-role port.

On attachment of an unsupported peripheral, including a hub on a system that doesn't support hubs, a Targeted Host system shouldn't fail silently but should provide a message or other indicator to inform the user that the host doesn't support the device.

This chapter focuses on Embedded Hosts and the host capabilities of OTG systems. Chapter 11 has more about using the unique capabilities of OTG ports.

Requirements

The ports in an Embedded Host system function much like ports in conventional PCs but without the need to support the bus speeds and bus currents that the targeted peripherals don't use. Table 2-1 compares the requirements for Embedded Host ports and conventional host ports.

Capability or Feature	Conventional Host	USB 2.0 Embedded Host
Communicate at high speed	Yes	Must support all devices on the Targeted Peripheral List. May support high, full, and low speeds; high and full speeds; full and low speeds; full speed only; or low speed only.
Communicate at full speed	Yes	
Communicate at low speed	Yes	
Support external hubs	Yes	Optional
Provide Targeted Peripheral List	No	Yes
Minimum available bus current per port	500 mA (100 mA if battery-powered)	8 mA or the amount needed by targeted peripherals, whichever is greater
OK to turn off VBUS when unneeded?	No	Yes
Connector	1 or more Standard-A receptacles	1 or more Standard-A receptacles

Table 2-1: USB 2.0 embedded hosts have different requirements compared to conventional USB 2.0 hosts.

An Embedded Host system can support just about any combination of speeds needed for the targeted peripherals. If all of the targeted peripherals use low speed or all use full speed, the system needs to support only one speed. A system that supports high speed must also support full speed. All host ports should support the same speeds and devices. The *On-The-Go and Embedded Host* supplement applies to the USB 2.0 specification and thus offers no specific guidance for USB embedded hosts on SuperSpeed systems.

Switching Off Bus Power

To lengthen battery life, embedded systems that use battery power typically conserve power when possible. Unlike conventional USB hosts, Embedded Host systems have the option to turn off VBUS to save power when the bus is idle.

When VBUS is off, the host needs a way to detect device attachment, and already attached devices need a way to signal that they want to communicate on the bus. Two protocols, the Attach Detection Protocol and the Session Request Protocol, meet these needs.

Attach Detection Protocol

Conventional hosts detect device attachment by monitoring for a voltage change on the D+ or D- data line. But the USB 2.0 specification forbids devices from powering the pull-up resistor on D+ or D- when VBUS is absent except to do data-line pulsing for the Session Request Protocol as described below. The Attach Detection Protocol (ADP) provides a way for a host to detect device attachment when VBUS is absent.

An Embedded Host or OTG system performs ADP probing by discharging the VBUS line, then measuring the time required for a known current to charge the line to a known voltage. If the line doesn't charge within the expected time, no device is present. The probing repeats about every 1.75 s. Host support for ADP is optional. Hubs don't support ADP probing, so if a hub lies between the host and device, the host can't use ADP probing.

Session Request Protocol

If the host has turned off VBUS, a device can use the Session Request Protocol (SRP) to request restoring VBUS.

A device requests the host to restore VBUS by performing data-line pulsing, which consists of switching in the pull-up on D+ (for full and high speed) or D- (for low speed) for 5–10 ms. The host detects the voltage. Hubs don't recognize SRP signaling, so if a hub lies between the host and device, the device can't use SRP.

An Embedded Host or OTG system that ever turns off VBUS with a series-A plug inserted must support SRP.

Functioning as a USB Device

An embedded system with USB host support can also provide a device port and function as a USB device. For example, a data logger might have a host port that connects to a drive for saving data and a device port that connects to a PC for uploading data. Unlike OTG systems, which can perform only one function at a time, a system with conventional host and device ports can function as a host and device at the same time.

Necessary Hardware

To function as a USB host, an embedded system must have a system processor, a USB host controller, a root hub, one or more host receptacles, and a power source (Figure 2-2).

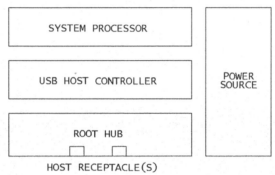

Figure 2-2. A USB host consists of a processor, USB host controller, root hub, one or more USB host receptacles, and a power source.

System Processor

The system processor is a microcontroller or other processor chip that executes the system's firmware. As explained later in this chapter, the choice of processor depends in part on the needed performance for USB communications.

USB Host Controller

The host-controller hardware includes electrical interfaces for one or more host ports and logic to implement low-level host protocols. The hardware can be in the system-processor chip or on a dedicated chip that interfaces to the system processor.

The electrical interface is one or more transceivers (for USB 2.0) or transmitters and receivers (for SuperSpeed) that interface to connectors.

17

The host controller's internal logic handles functions such as generating transactions to send data provided by the system onto the bus, making data received in transactions available to the system, error checking, and other tasks detailed in Chapter 8 of the USB 2.0 or USB 3.0 specification.

Root Hub

The root hub provides an interface between the host controller and its port(s). A root hub performs the same functions as external USB hubs, but the interface to the host controller is specific to the host hardware.

Host Connectors

Ports that function only as hosts ports use the same Standard-A receptacles that PCs use (Figure 2-3).

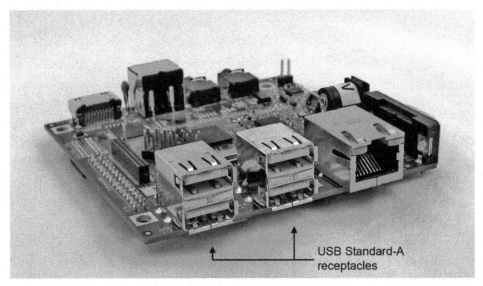

USB Standard-A
receptacles

Figure 2-3. The BeagleBoard-xM has four Standard-A host receptacles.

A system can have one or more host ports.

Designers of products that have both Standard-A (host) and type-B (device) receptacles should use product design, labeling, and product literature to inform users of the product's function. In particular, the product's design and labeling should make it clear that the product isn't a hub.

Source of Bus Current

The USB host provides a nominal +5V to all devices that attach directly to the host ports. Embedded Host ports must be capable of providing 8 mA or the amount of bus current the supported devices need, whichever is greater. Devices that attach to an external hub receive power from the hub. A standard hub can supply 100 mA per port if bus powered (150 mA for SuperSpeed) or 500 mA per port if self powered (900 mA for SuperSpeed).

What the Host Does

The motivation for developing the USB interface was to make it easy to use peripherals of all kinds on conventional PCs. To keep the cost of devices low, the host is responsible for managing the bus, including scheduling traffic and providing and managing power. Devices just need to respond to communications and other events initiated by the host and upstream hubs.

On some USB embedded host platforms, the OS or a host module handles many of the USB host functions. On other platforms, the developer must provide firmware for these tasks.

Detecting and Enumerating Devices

A host or hub detects an attached device by monitoring the voltage on the data lines and optionally by using the Attach Detection Protocol as described above. Hubs use control and interrupt transfers to inform the host of newly attached devices. On detecting a device, the host attempts to enumerate the device and assign a driver.

Supporting External Hubs

A USB embedded host can support external hubs or require all devices to attach directly to a host port. A host that supports hubs can support the hub class, including providing 500 mA to bus-powered hubs and supporting five tiers of hubs (Figure 2-4), or the host can support specific hub models.

Managing Traffic

The host schedules traffic on the bus, reserving time for endpoints that have guaranteed bandwidth and scheduling other traffic in the time that remains.

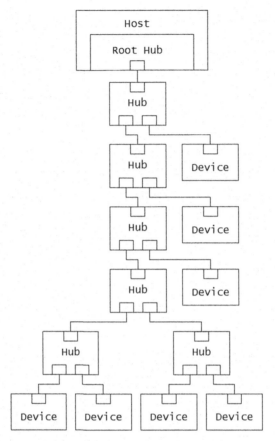

Figure 2-4. With support for the hub class, a host can have five tiers of external hubs.

Managing Power

During enumeration, a device's configuration descriptor requests bus current from the host. If the requested current isn't available, the host refuses to configure the device. To conserve power when the bus has no traffic, a host can use bus-signaling protocols to request devices to enter the Suspend state and reduce their use of bus current. When in the Suspend state, devices can use the remote wakeup protocol to request communications with the host. Embedded Host systems that are supplying bus power can remove power from the bus when the bus is idle.

Communicating with Devices

The ultimate purpose of a USB host is to exchange data with devices. The devices may belong to USB classes or use vendor-defined protocols.

Choosing a Development Platform

Because of the host's many responsibilities, adding USB host capability to a small embedded system may seem like a daunting task. Fortunately, a variety of hardware and programming platforms can ease the way.

Comparing Options

Host hardware and software are available for just about any need. Systems that need capabilities comparable to conventional PCs can use high-end processors targeted to embedded applications. Cost-sensitive systems that need good performance can use mid-range microcontrollers with USB host support either on-chip or in an external controller. Where high performance isn't essential, even 8-bit microcontrollers can access USB devices by interfacing to host modules that manage USB protocols.

The amount and type of programming the developer needs to provide host communications varies widely depending on the host hardware and the amount and type of firmware support for host communications. If you need to write USB host code from the ground up, the Linux source code for USB host communications can provide a model.

Table 2-2 compares options for implementing an Embedded Host port in an embedded system.

System Type	Sources	Host Communications Support
Embedded PC with host controller	beagleboard.org, Digi International Inc., EMAC, Inc.	Linux or Windows API, other protocols supported by the OS and programming environment
General-purpose microcontroller with on-chip host controller	Cypress Semiconductor, Freescale Semiconductor Inc., Microchip Technology, Texas Instruments	Libraries from chip provider

Table 2-2: Many hardware options are available for implementing hosts in embedded systems. (Part 1 of 2)

System Type	Sources	Host Communications Support
External host interface chip plus general-purpose microcontroller	PLX Technology, Maxim Integrated Products, Inc., ST-Ericsson	Libraries from chip provider
Processor with on-chip host module	FTDI (Vinculum II)	Vendor-specific API
Host module with interface to external processor	FTDI (Vinculum II in Vincil mode)	Vendor-specific command set
Processor with USB host and support for .NET Micro Framework and USB host communications	GHI Electronics	.NET Micro Framework classes

Table 2-2: Many hardware options are available for implementing hosts in embedded systems. (Part 2 of 2)

Embedded PC

At its heart, USB is an interface for PCs, and PC OSes such as Linux and Windows have rich support for USB host communications. An embedded PC can take advantage of this built-in support by using a distribution or edition of a PC OS targeted to small systems.

In an embedded PC, applications can access devices in much the same way that applications access devices on conventional PCs. The OS manages enumeration and other low-level protocols and provides drivers for popular USB device classes.

With an embedded PC, you can use many of the same development tools you use when developing mainstream PC applications. You can buy boards with Linux or Windows installed, or you can install an OS on suitable hardware.

Sources for embedded PCs with Linux or Windows installed include Digi International Inc. and EMAC, Inc. Chapter 3 has more about a Linux USB Embedded Host system that uses the BeagleBoard-xM open development board.

General-purpose Processor

A general-purpose microcontroller or other processor with an on-chip host controller allows full control of the firmware with low per-unit cost. The down side is the effort needed to program host communications. Firmware typically manages device detecting and enumeration, communications down to the transaction level, and bus power.

Chip vendors often provide firmware libraries that implement basic host communications and provide a foundation for application programming.

Sources for microcontrollers and processors with on-chip host controllers include Cypress Semiconductor, Freescale Semiconductor Inc., Microchip Technology, and Texas Instruments.

A microcontroller or other processor that doesn't have an on-chip USB host controller can use an external host interface chip. For example, ST-Ericsson's ISP1763A host controller can use an 8- or 16-bit bus interface to a system processor. Other sources for host interface chips are Maxim Integrated Products, Inc. and PLX Technology.

Host Module

For projects that don't have the firmware resources to support USB protocols, a USB host module can be a solution. The module manages enumeration and low-level communications and supports commands or an API for accessing popular device types. FTDI's Vinculum II is a host module with built-in support for accessing drives, keyboards, and other devices.

The Vinculum II has an on-chip processor core that supports an API for accessing USB devices. FTDI provides a C compiler for the processor. Supported USB device classes includes mass storage, hub, HID, still image, and audio. The module can also communicate with FTDI's FT232x USB UART devices.

The Vinculum II also supports an alternate mode that can use an asynchronous serial (UART), SPI, or parallel interface to an external processor. The processor uses defined commands to exchange data with USB devices. The Vinculum II handles the USB protocols and communications. This mode emulates the first-generation Vinculum.

For more on how to use the Vinculum II, download the free ebook *Embedded USB Design By Example* by John Hyde from *usb-by-example.com*.

Processor with .NET Micro Framework

Microsoft's .NET Framework is a popular programming framework for Windows applications written in .NET languages such as Visual C#. If you want to program in Visual C# but don't need the capabilities of even an embedded edition of Windows, GHI Electronics offers a series of boards with a system processor, a USB host controller, and built-in support for the .NET Micro Framework with .NET classes that support USB host communications. You can program the boards using the same Visual Studio software used to develop applications for PCs.

For more about USB host programming with the .NET Micro Framework, see the *Beginners Guide to NETMF* and other documentation for the GHI Electronics NETMF library at *ghielectronics.com*.

A Word about Protocol Analyzers

When developing a USB host system, no matter what hardware and programming platform you use, a USB protocol analyzer will save you time and trouble. A hardware-based protocol analyzer captures traffic and events on a bus segment and sends the information to a PC for decoding and displaying.

With this type of analyzer, you don't need to guess, wonder, or set up other debugging tools to try to find out what is happening. You can see the contents of every packet the host and device send. You know if the host sent what you expected and how the device responded. Monitoring traffic on a conventional host can be a rich source of clues for developing and debugging host communications for embedded systems.

Hardware-based protocol analyzers are available from multiple sources in a range of prices.

Software-only analyzers, which run on the host system, can be useful though they can show only what the host's drivers see, not transaction-level data on the bus. Chapter 3 shows how to use the usbmon software analyzer on Linux systems.

Non-USB Alternatives

Perhaps it's heresy to say this in a book about USB hosts, but not every embedded system needs USB host capability. Microcontrollers and application processors typically have a variety of I/O interfaces available. Before you decide to add a USB host port, it makes sense to decide if your system really needs one.

Many microcontrollers have serial interfaces such as a UART, SPI, and I²C, which can handle many tasks that require low to moderate throughput. For accessing a network, on-board Ethernet or wireless-network ports are alternatives. A system that needs to exchange data with PCs can use a USB device port with an appropriate driver for the desired task.

With that said, USB hosts are powerful and flexible system components, and peripherals with USB ports dominate the market. If your system needs to access peripherals, chances are good that a USB host is the way to go.

3

Using Linux
in Embedded Systems

This chapter introduces a development platform for a Linux embedded system that offers a middle ground between building a system from scratch and buying a fully configured system. You have to do some of the initial work yourself, but you gain a system that is capable and flexible.

Getting Started

The Linux OS requires a powerful processor architecture such as ARM, IA-32 (x86), or PowerPC. Providers of Linux-capable processors include Atmel Corporation, Freescale Semiconductor, Intel Corporation, and Texas Instruments.

A Linux distribution provides the software components for a complete, functional system. The Linux kernel is the heart of the system and manages system processes. A root file system provides a directory tree for files. Device drivers manage communications with hardware, including USB host controllers and USB devices. A bootloader program loads the OS on power up. Utilities enable configuring the system and testing. Applications support popular tasks such as text editing and web browsing.

Figure 3-1. The BeagleBoard-xM includes USB host ports, an OTG port, and an on-board USB/Ethernet adapter.

The BeagleBoard-xM Platform

The BeagleBoard-xM is a 3.5 in^2 board with four USB host ports, an OTG port, and the resources to support Linux and other OSes (Figure 3-1). The application processor is a Texas Instruments DM3730 ARM Cortex A8. ARM Cortex is a high-performance processor architecture with small code size, small silicon area, and low power consumption.

The BeagleBoard-xM is intended as a development platform for experimenting rather than for use in final products. Code developed for the board is portable to other hardware.

The BeagleBoard-xM is a second generation board with enhanced USB host support compared to the original BeagleBoard. The DM3730 processor contains a high-speed USB host subsystem and a high-speed USB OTG controller. Also on board are an SMSC LAN9514 USB 2.0 hub with four host ports and an embedded USB/Ethernet bridge.

The board has four USB Standard-A receptacles for attaching USB peripherals and a Mini-AB receptacle that can attach to a USB host, peripheral, or other OTG system. The host ports and the OTG port support low, full, and high speeds. Other on-board connectors are DVI-D, Ethernet, JTAG, S-video, stereo in and out, RS-232, LCD headers, and a camera header.

Unlike many embedded systems that store their program code in on-board flash memory, the BeagleBoard-xM executes its firmware from a micro-SD card inserted in the on-board receptacle. The micro-SD card included with the board contains a demo version of the Ångström distribution of Linux.

Even if the final project doesn't need a full-screen display, keyboard, and mouse, these devices can be useful during project development. A USB keyboard and mouse can attach to USB host ports. You can attach a monitor to the BeagleBoard-xM's DVI-D connector or use a monitor with a USB interface as described in Chapter 11.

With a display and keyboard, you can load and run applications much as you would on a conventional Linux PC. You can write and compile applications on the board or write applications on a PC, cross-compile for the BeagleBoard-xM, and copy the executable file to the board. A network connection can transfer files between the development PC and the BeagleBoard-xM.

Linux is just one option for the BeagleBoard-xM, which can also run embedded editions of Windows, Android, other OSes, or other firmware. For details about how to obtain a BeagleBoard-xM and get it up and running, visit *beagleboard.org*.

Selecting a Distribution

Using an established distribution is a way to get a Linux system working quickly. Distributions suitable for smaller systems include Ubuntu Netbook (*ubuntu.com*) and the Ångström distribution (*www.angstrom-distribution.org*). Either of these distributions plus additional drivers and user applications can fit on a 4GB SD card.

Ubuntu Netbook is a full-featured OS optimized for devices with small screens. (Beginning with Ubuntu 11.04, PC netbooks use Ubuntu's Desktop edition, but the OMAP arm architecture continues to use Ubuntu Netbook.) The distribution provides drivers for accessing a variety of USB devices and thus can be a good platform for experimenting. Links to images and installation instructions for a variety of Ubuntu distributions, including Ubuntu Netbook, are at *elinux.org/BeagleBoard-Ubuntu*.

I tested the Linux code in this book using the preinstalled OMAP3 armel image for Ubuntu Netbook 11.04 (Natty Narwhal) from the URL above. The distribution uses the Unity Desktop. If you use a different Linux distribution or Desktop GUI, some features may be in different locations.

If you would like a leaner distribution, the demo Ångström distribution that ships with the BeagleBoard-xM is an option. You can download and install additional components, including USB device drivers, from Ångström's package server.

For a distribution that provides the components your system needs and nothing more, you can create your own. OpenEmbedded (*openembedded.org*) is a build framework whose BitBake tool manages the compiling and linking of source code to build custom images.

Another option is the Narcissus image builder (*narcissus.angstrom-distribution.org*), which provides a web interface for creating a distribution using compiled code from the Ångström repository.

How to use Linux is a book-length topic in itself. For a detailed guide to using Linux in embedded systems, two good books are *Embedded Linux Primer* by Christopher Hallinan (Prentice Hall) and *Pro Linux Embedded Systems* by Gene Sally (Apress).

Obtaining Additional Software

No matter what distribution you use, you will likely need to install additional applications, drivers, or other software to support needed functions.

Ubuntu's Advanced Packaging Tool (APT) automates the tasks of obtaining, configuring, and installing software packages. The Synaptic Package Manager (**System Settings > System > Synaptic Package Manager**) provides a graphical interface for searching for, downloading, and installing software packages using the APT.

From a command line, you can use the `apt-get` tool to download and install software. This command updates the local package index:

`sudo apt-get update`

To download and install a package, enter:

`sudo apt-get install` *package_name*

where *package_name* is the name of the desired package.

You can browse or search for packages from *packages.ubuntu.com*.

Packages are available from a variety of repositories. If something you're interested in doesn't seem to be available, you may need to expand the search. In Synaptic Package Manager, select **Settings > Repositories** and select the sources you would like to use. Or load `/etc/apt/sources.list` in a text editor and uncomment the repositories you would like to add.

For more on using `apt-get`, enter `apt-get help`.

The Ångström distribution provides the opkg package management tool, which uses similar syntax to apt-get.

Creating and Running Applications

Whatever platform you use, you'll need to know how to compile and run applications. Below is one way to create, compile, and run basic applications on a Beagle-Board-xM with Linux.

Using the Command Line

Users of conventional PCs often do everything they need from the graphical user interface (GUI), but developers for embedded systems are likely to use the command line for at least some tasks. Systems that don't need a GUI can boot to a shell that provides a command line. On GUI systems, you can use a command line in a terminal-emulator application such as **gnome-terminal.** Look for a **Terminal** application in **Applications**. A good guide to the Linux command line is *Beginning the Linux Command Line* by Sander van Vugt (Apress).

Obtaining a Toolchain

To develop applications, you will need a toolchain. A typical toolchain contains a compiler, libraries, an assembler, a linker and a debugger. A library such as the GNU C library (*gnu.org/software/libc*) provides support for input/output, memory management, string manipulation, and other common tasks.

The Ångström distribution and CodeSourcery (*codesourcery.com*) are sources for C compilers and toolchains for the BeagleBoard-xM. You can work from a command line or use an integrated development environment (IDE) such as Eclipse (*eclipse.org*).

A compiler creates executable code for a particular computer architecture. With a cross compiler, you can use a PC to compile applications for an embedded system that uses a different architecture.

To use a Linux PC to compile applications for the BeagleBoard-xM, download and install an armv7a toolchain for your PC from Ångström, CodeSourcery, or another source. Windows PCs can run Linux in a virtual machine using virtualization software such as VMWare's VMware Player.

To add the compiler's location to the system-wide path, append the location to the PATH statement in the /etc/environment file.

For the Ångström toolchain, the location of the `arm-angstrom-linux-gnueabi-gcc` compiler is:

your_installation_directory/angstrom/arm/bin

where *your_installation_directory* is the path where you installed the compiler.

For CodeSourcery_Lite the location of the `arm-none-linux-gnueabi-gcc` compiler is:

your_installation_directory/CodeSourcery_G++_Lite/bin

where again *your_installation_directory* is the path where you installed the compiler.

This PATH statement includes the path to a compiler at `/usr/local/angstrom/arm/bin`:

PATH="/usr/local/bin:/usr/bin:/bin:/usr/local/angstrom/arm/bin"

For the changes in the path to take effect, log out and back in.

Writing and Compiling

You can write source code on a PC using a text editor or an IDE such as Eclipse. Here is a classic first application:

```
#include <stdio.h>

int main()
{
    printf("Hello, world.\n");
}
```

Save the source code above in a file titled *helloworld.c*.

To compile from the command line, provide the name of the source file and use the `-o` option to specify the desired name of the executable file.

To compile `helloworld.c` with the Ångström toolchain, use:

arm-angstrom-linux-gnueabi-gcc helloworld.c -o helloworld

For CodeSourcery, use:

arm-none-linux-gnueabi-gcc helloworld.c -o helloworld

These are the basics. For more on compiling applications, including how to use the `make` and `pkg-config` tools to build projects and how to compile using Eclipse or other IDEs, consult the tool's documentation

Running Applications

If the embedded system has a network connection to the development PC, you can use the `scp` command to transfer the compiled application from a PC to the embedded system:

```
scp helloworld jan@192.168.1.93:/home/jan/programs
```

For more on using `scp`, see Chapter 7.

Another option is to copy the file to a flash drive:

```
cp helloworld /media/Lexar/helloworld
```

then attach the drive to the BeagleBoard and move the file from the flash drive to the BeagleBoard:

```
mv /media/Lexar/helloworld helloworld
```

For more on how to access flash drives, see Chapter 5.

After transferring the file, you can run the application from a command line on the target system. From the directory that contains the executable file, run the application, preceding the filename with `./` to indicate the current directory:

```
./helloworld
```

The terminal's screen should display:

```
Hello, world.
```

Issues for Embedded Systems

Although embedded Linux systems have much in common with conventional Linux systems, small systems have needs that are less common on conventional systems. Issues that are likely to come up when programming Linux-based embedded systems are how to log in automatically, setting permissions to run programs without a password, and running applications at startup.

Logging In Automatically

Many embedded systems need to start without waiting for a user to log in. A solution is to set up the system to log in automatically. In Ubuntu's Unity Desktop, select **System Settings > System > Login Screen** or run `gdmsetup` at a command line. Click **Unlock**, enter the administrative password, and follow the prompts to enable a user to log in automatically on bootup.

Setting Permissions

One way to manage permissions is to log in as root, guaranteeing administrative privileges for all tasks. But for safety and security, many systems boot to user accounts.

These systems may need to run some code with administrative privileges without asking for a password. The sudoers file and udev rules provide ways to do so.

Running a Program without Supplying a Password

To remove the need to enter a password, you can add an entry to the sudoers file. The visudo editor program loads the sudoers file and checks for errors and provides other safeguards when you edit the file. To start visudo, enter:

```
sudo visudo
```

To enable the user jan to run the program /usr/bin/my_app without supplying a password, add this line to the file:

```
jan ALL=NOPASSWD: /usr/local/bin/my_app
```

ALL specifies that the entry applies to all servers in the network.

NOPASSWD means that the user can run the named application without providing a password.

/usr/local/bin/my_app is the application and its path.

The sudoers man page has more examples and options.

Using Rules to Grant Permissions

To enable users without administrative privileges to access a device that requires administrative privileges, you can create a udev rule that sets permissions. The udev subsystem uses files that have the extension .rules and contain plain-text rules for managing the device nodes in the /dev directory. (Chapter 4 has more about device nodes.)

The default locations for the rules files are the /lib/udev/rules.d and /etc/udev/rules.d directories. A file in /etc/udev/rules.d overrides any file with the same name in /lib/udev/rules.d. The OS reads the files in ascending numerical order by name, followed by files whose names begin with a letter. For example, 60-persistent-storage.rules is processed before 80-drivers.rules, which is processed before myrule.rules.

You can create udev rules as needed for specific devices. For example, as Chapter 10 explains, applications that use the libusb library to access a device require administrative privileges by default. A udev rule can enable users without administrative privileges to run the application.

This rule identifies the USB device with Vendor ID = 0925h and Product ID = 1456h and sets the MODE parameter to grant read/write permissions for all users:

```
SUBSYSTEM=="usb", ATTR{idVendor}=="0925", ATTR{idProduct}=="1456",
    MODE="0666"
```

Place the above rule in a file with a `.rules` extension (such as `81-libusb.rules`) and save the file in `/etc/udev/rules.d`. On the next bootup, users can run applications that use `libusb` functions to read and write to the specified device.

To find the attributes and other information to use in a rule for a device node, use the `udevadm` tool:

udevadm info --attribute-walk --name=/dev/bus/usb/*xxx*/*yyy*

where *xxx* is the desired bus number in `/dev/bus/usb` and *yyy* is the desired device number in `/dev/bus/usb/*xxx*`. For example:

udevadm info --attribute-walk --name=/dev/bus/usb/001/002

To find a device's bus and device number, use the `lsusb` command as described in Chapter 4.

The tool displays information for the specified device followed by information about all upstream hubs and the host controller. Listing 3-1 shows a portion of the command's output with information about a vendor-defined device, including the SUB-SYSTEM and ATTR values used in the rule above.

```
looking at device '/devices/platform/ehci-omap.0/usb1/1-2/1-2.2':
  KERNEL=="1-2.2"
  SUBSYSTEM=="usb"
  DRIVER=="usb"
  ATTR{configuration}==""
  ATTR{bNumInterfaces}==" 1"
  ATTR{bConfigurationValue}=="1"
  ATTR{bmAttributes}=="c0"
  ATTR{bMaxPower}=="100mA"
  ATTR{urbnum}=="12"
  ATTR{idVendor}=="0925"
  ATTR{idProduct}=="1456"
  ATTR{bcdDevice}=="0001"
  ATTR{bDeviceClass}=="00"
  ATTR{bDeviceSubClass}=="00"
  ATTR{bDeviceProtocol}=="00"
  ATTR{bNumConfigurations}=="1"
  ATTR{bMaxPacketSize0}=="8"
  ATTR{speed}=="12"
```

Listing 3-1: The udevadm tool displays attributes and other information about devices. (Part 1 of 2)

```
ATTR{busnum}=="1"
ATTR{devnum}=="4"
ATTR{devpath}=="2.2"
ATTR{version}==" 2.00"
ATTR{maxchild}=="0"
ATTR{quirks}=="0x0"
ATTR{avoid_reset_quirk}=="0"
ATTR{authorized}=="1"
ATTR{manufacturer}=="Lakeview Research"
ATTR{product}=="WinUSB Demo"
```

Listing 3-1: The udevadm tool displays attributes and other information about devices. (Part 2 of 2)

A rule can also grant permissions to users in a specified group. This example grants read/write permissions for a device to users in the group winusb.

```
SUBSYSTEM=="usb", ATTR{idVendor}=="0925", ATTR{idProduct}=="1456",
    MODE:="0660", GROUP="winusb"
```

To view the groups a user belongs to, use the groups command:

groups jan

The *LED Indicators* section below in this chapter shows how to use a udev rule to grant user permissions to control the BeagleBoard-xM's on-board LEDs. Chapter 5 shows how udev rules can control whether the OS automatically mounts USB drives on attachment. For more about udev, see the man pages for udev, udevadm, and groups. For more about file permissions, see the man page for chmod.

Running an Application at Startup

On startup, embedded systems typically run an application to perform the device's function. For example, a data logger might run a program to collect and store data periodically.

OSes with GUIs typically provide a way to specify programs to run on bootup. In Ubuntu's Unity Desktop, you can enter commands to run programs under **System Settings > Personal > Startup Applications**.

To run /usr/local/bin/my_app, enter this command as a startup application:

/usr/local/bin/my_app

If the application requires administrative privileges, edit the sudoers file as described above to enable the application to run without a password.

Then add `sudo` to the startup command:

sudo /usr/local/bin/my_app

You can also run an application from within a terminal. This command runs gnome-terminal, which in turn runs /usr/local/bin/my_app:

gnome-terminal -e "sudo /usr/local/bin/my_app"

Another way to run a program on startup is to place a command that runs a startup application in the /etc/rc.local file, which executes after other startup scripts but before the login prompt.

rc.local must be executable. Change the file's permissions to make it executable if needed:

sudo chmod +x rc.local

This entry in rc.local runs /usr/local/bin/my_app:

/usr/local/bin/my_app

Add "&" to cause the application to run as a background task:

/usr/local/bin/my_app &

rc.local runs as root, so you don't need to set permissions to run an application from the file.

An application that doesn't run from a terminal or GUI might not have an obvious way to close the application. Use the pidof command to find the application's process number:

pidof my_app
1024

Kill the process by providing its number:

kill 1024

Providing Data for Debugging

For testing and debugging, two common ways for an embedded system to provide status information are writing messages to a terminal and toggling LEDs. The examples in this book use these methods.

Messages

Applications that run from a shell or terminal emulator can use printf statements to display messages.

A statement can provide a basic text message to indicate status:

printf("Data written to the file.\n");

Or a statement can display the values of variables. This statement displays the error string returned by the cupsLastErrorString function:

```
printf("status = %s\n", cupsLastErrorString());
```

printf can also send messages to a remote terminal connected via a serial port or other interface. Chapter 7 shows how to send messages via a USB virtual serial port.

LED Indicators

A classic test application for embedded systems involves toggling LEDs. For example, to demonstrate reading from a flash drive, firmware can read a file containing commands to turn LEDs on or off.

Recent Linux kernels support an led class. Each LED that supports the led class functions has a directory. The BeagleBoard-xM has two user LEDs in these directories:

```
/sys/devices/platform/leds-gpio/leds/beagleboard::usr0
/sys/devices/platform/leds-gpio/leds/beagleboard::usr1
```

Each LED also has a symbolic link that points to the LED's directory:

```
/sys/class/leds/beagleboard::usr0
/sys/class/leds/beagleboard::usr1
```

From the directories or their symbolic links, you can access virtual files that contain attributes that control an LED's function and operation.

By default, the OS requires administrative privileges to control the LEDs. A udev rule can grant user permissions to control the LEDs. Create a file called 90-leds.rules and copy this rule into it:

```
SUBSYSTEM=="leds", PROGRAM+="/bin/sh -c 'chmod a+rw
    /sys/devices/platform/leds-gpio/leds/beagleboard::usr0/trigger
    /sys/devices/platform/leds-gpio/leds/beagleboard::usr0/brightness
    /sys/devices/platform/leds-gpio/leds/beagleboard::usr1/trigger
    /sys/devices/platform/leds-gpio/leds/beagleboard::usr1/brightness'"
```

The rule should be on a single line in the file. (Press **Enter** only at the end of the rule.) Save the file in the /etc/udev/rules.d directory.

The rule runs a shell program (/bin/sh), passing a string that contains a command to execute. The chmod a+rw command grants read/write permissions to all users for the trigger and brightness attributes for each LED.

The functions below shows how to initialize and toggle the LEDs.

The functions use the include statements in Listing 3-2.

```
#include <stdio.h>
#include <string.h>
```

Listing 3-2: The LED functions use these include statements.

Initializing the LEDs

Each LED has a trigger file that can assign a kernel-based event to the LED. To view the supported events for usr0, at a command prompt, enter:

`cat /sys/class/leds/beagleboard::usr0/trigger`

The output shows the active event in square brackets:

`none nand-disk mmc0 [heartbeat]`

To see the same information for usr1, substitute usr1 for usr0 in the above command.

On boot-up, the default events for the BeagleBoard are heartbeat for usr0 and mmc0 for usr1. To enable using the LEDs for other purposes, set the events to none. As root, enter:

`echo none > /sys/class/leds/beagleboard::usr0/trigger`
`echo none > /sys/class/leds/beagleboard::usr1/trigger`

Or from a user account, enter:

`echo none | sudo tee > /sys/class/leds/beagleboard::usr0/trigger`
`echo none | sudo tee > /sys/class/leds/beagleboard::usr1/trigger`

You can also set the events in program code. Listing 3-3's function sets the events for both LEDs to none.

```
void led_initialize()
{
    int led_number;
    char* led_trigger[2];
    led_trigger[0] = "/sys/class/leds/beagleboard::usr0/trigger";
    led_trigger[1] = "/sys/class/leds/beagleboard::usr1/trigger";
    FILE *led_trigger_file = NULL;
    char trigger_none[] = "none";
```

Listing 3-3: This function initializes the LED events. (Part 1 of 2)

```
for (led_number = 0; led_number < 2; led_number++)
{
    if ((led_trigger_file = fopen(led_trigger[led_number], "r+")) !=
        NULL)
    {
        fwrite(
            trigger_none, sizeof(trigger_none), sizeof(char),
                led_trigger_file);
        fclose(led_trigger_file);
    }
}
}
```

Listing 3-3: This function initializes the LED events. (Part 2 of 2)

The led_trigger array contains the paths to the two trigger files.

A for loop steps through the LEDs.

fopen opens the specified LED's trigger file for reading and writing and returns a pointer to the file.

frwrite writes "none" to the trigger file, and fclose closes the file.

Turning the LEDs On and Off

Each LED has a brightness file that can turn the LED on or off.

To view the current state of the brightness file for usr0, at a command prompt, enter:

cat /sys/class/leds/beagleboard::usr0/brightness

The output is zero (off) or 1 (on).

To see the same information for usr1, substitute usr1 for usr0 in the above command.

To turn an LED off or on, echo 0 or 1 to the file. As root, enter:

echo 0 > /sys/class/leds/beagleboard::usr0/brightness
echo 1 > /sys/class/leds/beagleboard::usr1/brightness

Or from a user account, enter:

echo 0 | sudo tee > /sys/class/leds/beagleboard::usr0/brightness
echo 1 | sudo tee > /sys/class/leds/beagleboard::usr1/brightness

You can also turn the LEDs on and off in program code. Listing 3-4's function turns a specified LED on or off.

```
void led_control(int led_number, int led_state)
{
    char led_state_char[2];
    char* led_brightness[2];
    FILE *led_control_file = NULL;

    led_brightness[0] =
        "/sys/class/leds/beagleboard::usr0/brightness";
    led_brightness[1] =
        "/sys/class/leds/beagleboard::usr1/brightness";

    if ((led_control_file =
        fopen(led_brightness[led_number], "r+")) != NULL)
    {
        sprintf(led_state_char, "%d", led_state);
        fwrite(led_state_char, sizeof(char), 1, led_control_file);
        fclose(led_control_file);
    }
}
```

Listing 3-4: This function turns a specified LED on or off.

The function accepts an LED number and LED state. The led_number parameter is 0 or 1. The led_state parameter is 0 for off and 1 for on.

led_state_char holds the LED state as a null-terminated char array.

The led_brightness array contains the paths to the two brightness files.

fopen opens the specified LED's brightness file for reading and appending and returns a pointer to the file.

sprintf converts the passed led_state to a char and stores the result in a null-terminated char array, frwrite writes the char to the brightness file, and fclose closes the file.

To turn both LEDs off, call the function with these parameters:

```
led_control(0, 0);
led_control(1, 0);
```

To turn both LEDs on, use:

```
led_control(0, 1);
led_control(1, 1);
```

Using the Functions

You can copy the above functions directly into an application file, or you can place the functions in their own file and use a header file and include statement to add the functions to an application.

To use a separate file, create a file called led_control.c and copy the contents of Listing 3-2, Listing 3-3, and Listing 3-4 into the file. Create a file called led_control.h and copy Listing 3-5's text into it:

```
#include "led_control.c"

#ifndef LED_CONTROL_H_
#define LED_CONTROL_H_

void led_control(int led_number, int led_state);
void led_initialize();

#endif
```

Listing 3-5: The LED control code uses this header file.

In code that uses the LED functions, include led_control.h. See Chapter 6 for an example that uses keypresses to control the LEDs.

4

Exploring USB in Linux

This chapter introduces tools and techniques for exploring USB devices in embedded Linux systems. You'll learn how to obtain information about attached USB devices and how to view USB traffic for debugging.

Learning about Attached Devices

The home for USB support under Linux is the Linux USB project at *linux-usb.org*. Among the site's offerings are a list of known working devices, a programming guide for USB drivers, and a link to the Linux USB email list.

Linux commands can provide useful information about attached USB devices and how they communicate.

Viewing Device Information

The lsusb command lists attached and available USB devices. To see all devices, at a command prompt, enter:

```
lsusb
```

Here is example output from a system with seven devices:

```
Bus 001 Device 007: ID 05dc:a813 Lexar Media, Inc.
Bus 001 Device 006: ID 0461:4d22 Primax Electronics, Ltd
```

```
Bus 001 Device 005: ID 413c:2005 Dell Computer Corp. RT7D50 Keyboard
Bus 001 Device 004: ID 0403:6001 Future Technology Devices International,
    Ltd FT232 USB-Serial (UART) IC
Bus 001 Device 003: ID 0424:ec00 Standard Microsystems Corp.
Bus 001 Device 002: ID 0424:9514 Standard Microsystems Corp.
Bus 001 Device 001: ID 1d6b:0002 Linux Foundation 2.0 root hub
```

For each device, the command lists the bus number, the device's address on the bus, the device's Vendor ID and Product ID, and the manufacturer's name. Some entries provide a description of the device.

The lsusb command can also show the contents of the descriptors for a specific device. This command displays descriptors for a device with Vendor ID 05dc and Product ID a813:

lsusb -d 05dc:a813 -v

Listing 4-1 shows the command's output. The descriptors shown are for a device with a mass-storage interface and two bulk endpoints.

```
Bus 001 Device 024: ID 05dc:a813 Lexar Media, Inc.
Device Descriptor:
    bLength                18
    bDescriptorType         1
    bcdUSB               2.00
    bDeviceClass            0 (Defined at Interface level)
    bDeviceSubClass         0
    bDeviceProtocol         0
    bMaxPacketSize0        64
    idVendor           0x05dc Lexar Media, Inc.
    idProduct          0xa813
    bcdDevice           30.00
    iManufacturer           1
    iProduct                2
    iSerial                 3
    bNumConfigurations      1
```

Listing 4-1: The lsusb command can display descriptors for a specified device such as this flash drive (Part 1 of 3).

```
Configuration Descriptor:
      bLength                 9
      bDescriptorType         2
      wTotalLength            32
      bNumInterfaces          1
      bConfigurationValue     1
      iConfiguration          0
      bmAttributes         0x80 (Bus Powered)
      MaxPower           100mA
      Interface Descriptor:
        bLength               9
        bDescriptorType       4
        bInterfaceNumber      0
        bAlternateSetting     0
        bNumEndpoints         2
        bInterfaceClass       8 Mass Storage
        bInterfaceSubClass    6 SCSI
        bInterfaceProtocol   80 Bulk (Zip)
        iInterface            0
        Endpoint Descriptor:
          bLength             7
          bDescriptorType     5
          bEndpointAddress 0x81  EP 1 IN
          bmAttributes        2
            Transfer Type          Bulk
            Synch Type             None
            Usage Type             Data
          wMaxPacketSize   0x0200  1x 512 bytes
          bInterval         255
```

Listing 4-1: The lsusb command can display descriptors for a specified device such as this flash drive (Part 2 of 3).

```
        Endpoint Descriptor:
          bLength                7
          bDescriptorType        5
          bEndpointAddress     0x02  EP 2 OUT
          bmAttributes           2
            Transfer Type             Bulk
            Synch Type                None
            Usage Type                Data
          wMaxPacketSize       0x0200  1x 512 bytes
          bInterval            255
```

Listing 4-1: The lsusb command can display descriptors for a specified device such as this flash drive (Part 3 of 3).

Another way to learn about attached devices is by exploring the contents of the sysfs virtual file system. Information about USB devices is in /sys/bus/usb/devices. To view the devices, at a command line, enter:

cd /sys/bus/usb/devices
sudo ls

The directory contains symbolic links that each point to a directory with information about a device, a device configuration or interface, or a root hub. An example listing is:

```
1-0:1.0  1-2  1-2.1  1-2:1.0  1-2.1:1.0  1-2.2  1-2.2:1.0  1-2.4
    1-2.4:1.0  1-2.5  1-2.5:1.0  usb1
```

To view the targets of the symbolic links, use ls -l.

Each symbolic link indicates the bus number and the position of the device on the bus. Values that follow ":" are the active configuration and interface as appropriate.

For example, 1-0:1.0 is the symbolic link for the device at bus 1, port 0 using configuration 1, interface 0. The link points to a directory of items with information about the interface. By examining the bInterfaceClass item, you can learn that bInterfaceClass = 09h, which indicates that the interface belongs to a hub:

cd /sys/bus/usb/devices/1-0:1.0
ls
```
bAlternateSetting bInterfaceNumber   bInterfaceSubClass driver modalias
    subsystem uevent
bInterfaceClass   bInterfaceProtocol bNumEndpoints      ep_81   power
    supports_autosuspend
```
cat bInterfaceClass
```
09
```

The driver directory and its subdirectories have information about the driver assigned to the interface. This command lists the drivers assigned to the hub:

```
cat /sys/bus/usb/devices/1-0:1.0/driver/module/drivers
usb:hub usb:usbfs
```

Dots indicate additional downstream hubs between a device and root hub. For example, the name `1-2.1:1.0` indicates that a downstream hub attaches to port 2 on the root hub, and port 1 on the downstream hub attaches to a device with active configuration 1, interface zero.

`usb1` is the symbolic link for the root hub on bus 1, the single bus in the example.

Using Device Nodes

A Linux device node is a virtual file that represents a device. The udev subsystem introduced in Chapter 3 creates device nodes from the information in sysfs (the `/sys` directory tree) and stores the device nodes in the `/dev` directory and its subdirectories. A single physical device can have multiple device nodes. For example, a drive may have one device node for the device (`/dev/sda`) and an additional node for each logical volume (`/dev/sda1`, `/dev/sda2`). Device nodes for mice and keyboards are in `/dev/input`.

Applications can use a device node to obtain access to some devices. Chapter 5 shows how an application can use a device node to find a drive's mount point, which the application can use to gain access to the drive. Chapter 7 shows how a USB virtual serial port can gain access to a virtual serial port by opening the port represented by its device node at `/dev/ttyUSB0`.

For many other devices, such as keyboards and mice, the OS or other libraries provide functions that enable applications to communicate with the devices without directly accessing the device nodes.

Drivers for USB Communications

To support communications with a USB device, a system must have a device driver to manage communications with the device and one or more drivers to manage communications between the device driver and the host-controller hardware.

The drivers can be compiled into the kernel or compiled as modules that are loaded on startup or as needed. Drivers for host controllers and other on-board hardware are typically compiled into the kernel. For devices that may come and go, such as USB drives, the OS might load the driver on attachment.

Host-controller Drivers

These are major USB host-controller drivers for Linux:

usbcore provides low-level support for USB communications that aren't specific to the hardware.

ehci_hcd supports host communications for EHCI (high-speed) host controllers.

ohci_hcd supports host communications for OHCI (low- and full-speed) host controllers. UHCI is an alternate host-controller architecture for low and full speeds, but embedded systems tend to use OHCI because it does more of the work in hardware and thus requires less software control.

Some host controllers use a controller-specific driver. For example, musb_hdrc is a driver for the Inventra high-speed dual-role controller (HDRC) controller, an ASIC design that the BeagleBoard-xM's processor uses for its OTG port.

Driver Modules

In Ubuntu and many other Linux distributions, the loadable kernel driver modules are in this directory:

/lib/modules/*kernel_version*/kernel/drivers

where **kernel_version** is the output of the uname -r command

For example, if uname -r returns 2.6.38-8-omap, the loadable driver modules are in:

/lib/modules/2.6.38-8-omap/kernel/drivers

Table 4-1 shows common locations of loadable modules for accessing USB devices and other USB-related communications in Linux.

Driver subdirectory	Devices
bluetooth	Bluetooth dongles
hid	HID-class devices
i2c/busses	I^2C adapters
isdn	ISDN controllers
media/dvb/dvb-usb	Digital video broadcasting (DVB) devices
media/IR	Infrared remote controls
media/video	Video devices. USB video-class devices are in media/video/uvc.
net/usb	CDC-class Ethernet adapters, network-based host-to-host adapters

Table 4-1: USB driver modules are in a variety of subdirectories under /lib/modules/<kernel version>/kernel/drivers. (Part 1 of 2)

Driver subdirectory	Devices
staging	Drivers that aren't ready to be included elsewhere in the main kernel tree for technical reasons
usb/atm	ADSL modems and other communications class devices that use asynchronous transfer mode
usb/c67x00	Cypress C67x00 OTG controllers
usb/class/cdc-acm	Devices that use the communications-class ACM protocol, including some USB virtual serial-port devices
usb/class/usblp	Printers
usb/class/usbtmc	Devices that use the USB test and measurement class
usb/gadget	Drivers to support the system's functioning as a USB device
usb/host	Support for specific host-controllers
usb/image	Scanners and image devices
usb/misc	Robot controllers, firmware loaders, USB displays, USB core testing, and other devices that don't fit another category
usb/mon	USB protocol analyzer
usb/otg	Support for specific OTG controller hardware
usb/serial	USB/serial adapters
usb/storage	Drives and other USB mass-storage devices
usb/wusbcore	Wireless USB

Table 4-1: USB driver modules are in a variety of subdirectories under /lib/modules/<kernel version>/kernel/drivers. (Part 2 of 2)

To view the modules currently loaded, enter:

`lsmod`

Listing 4-2 shows the output of the lsmod command on a system that has four USB devices with modules loaded.

Module	Size	Used by
usb_storage	43956	1
ftdi_sio	31778	0
smsc95xx	17508	0
usbserial	36196	1 ftdi_sio
usbnet	19666	1 smsc95xx
usbhid	44390	0
hid	79362	1 usbhid

Listing 4-2: The lsmod command displays the modules used by USB devices.

A flash drive uses the usb_storage module. A USB/serial adapter (FTDI FT232x USB UART) uses ftdi_sio, which in turn uses usbserial. A USB/Ethernet adapter (a built-in SMSC95XX USB 2.0 Ethernet Device) uses smsc95xx, which in turn uses usbnet. A HID keyboard uses hid, which uses usbhid.

The modprobe program can add or remove loadable kernel modules. For example, to load the usbmon driver to enable USB traffic monitoring, enter:

sudo modprobe usbmon

modprobe also detects and loads any dependencies a module requires.

Linux drivers are available for a wealth of devices. If you need to write a host driver for an unsupported device, the book *Linux Device Drivers* by Jonathan Corbet, Alessandro Rubini, and Greg Kroah-Hartman (O'Reilly Media) is a good resource.

Driver Attributes and Information

To enable setting and viewing driver attributes and to provide other information about the driver, each loaded module has a directory of virtual files under /sys/module.

Each virtual file holds an attribute or other piece of information about the module. The attributes vary with the driver. Some attributes are read only. Common attributes are refcnt, which contains the number of devices currently using the module, and initstate, which contains the initialization state of the module (live, coming, going).

The parameters directory contains driver-specific attributes. For example, because some USB drives need time to "settle" before being accessed, usb_storage has a delay_use parameter that sets the number of seconds between detecting and allowing access to USB storage devices.

A module's `drivers` directory contains symbolic links to the module's driver(s).

Monitoring Events on Attachment

The `dmesg` command can verify that a recently attached device installed correctly or display information about problems encountered. The command displays messages from the kernel's message buffer.

Listing 4-3 shows a portion of the `dmesg` output after attaching a USB/serial adapter.

```
[130980.041381] usb 1-2.2: new full speed USB device using ehci-omap and
    address 21
[130980.171813] ftdi_sio 1-2.2:1.0: FTDI USB Serial Device converter
    detected
[130980.171997] usb 1-2.2: Detected FT8U232AM
[130980.172027] usb 1-2.2: Number of endpoints 2
[130980.172027] usb 1-2.2: Endpoint 1 MaxPacketSize 64
[130980.172058] usb 1-2.2: Endpoint 2 MaxPacketSize 64
[130980.172058] usb 1-2.2: Setting MaxPacketSize 64
[130980.172698] ftdi_sio ttyUSB0: Unable to read latency timer: -32
[130980.173370] usb 1-2.2: FTDI USB Serial Device converter now attached
    to ttyUSB0
```

Listing 4-3: This output from the dmesg command displays information about a recently attached USB/serial adapter.

The output shows that the system detected an FTDI USB Serial Device converter with two endpoints, each with a maximum packet size of 64. The system assigned the converter to the device node `ttyUSB0`.

Monitoring USB Traffic

An advantage of Linux in embedded USB host systems is the tools available for monitoring USB traffic. The `usbmon` facility built into recent kernels can log USB traffic, and the `vusb-analyzer` application can decode `usbmon`'s log files and display them in a user-friendly format.

Getting and Using Text Logs

In Linux and other OSes, USB class and device drivers communicate with USB host controllers by submitting USB request blocks (URBs). Each URB requests to send or receive data to or from a specified endpoint on a device. The host controller schedules requests on the bus and notifies the driver when a request completes. The `usbmon` program can capture and display logs of USB traffic, including enumeration requests, at the URB level.

Logging uses the `debugfs` file system, which must be enabled in the Linux kernel configuration. To mount `debugfs`, enter:

```
mount -t debugfs none_debugs /sys/kernel/debug
```

If `usbmon` was built as a module (not built into the kernel), you also need to load the module:

```
sudo modprobe usbmon
```

You're now ready to log traffic. To display a log of all USB traffic, enter:

```
cat /sys/kernel/debug/usb/usbmon/0u
```

To stop logging, press `Ctrl+C`.

On systems with multiple buses, you can limit the logging to a single bus. Use `lsusb` as described above to find the bus number for the device you're interested in. To log traffic on bus 001, use:

```
cat /sys/kernel/debug/usb/usbmon/1u
```

In most cases, you'll want to redirect the output to a file to analyze. This command captures and saves a log in the file `usb1.mon`:

```
cat /sys/kernel/debug/usb/usbmon/0u > usb1.mon
```

The log file consists of lines of text with each line representing an URB submitted by a driver, an URB callback, or a submission error. A line consists of words of data separated by white space. The number and position of the words varies depending on the event type. Here is a line from a log showing a request for a device descriptor:

```
dedeb680 223163230 S Ci:1:008:0 s 80 06 0100 0000 0012 18 <
```

The log contains these words:

`dedeb680` is a tag that identifies the URB.

`223163230` is a timestamp in µs.

`S` indicates that the event is an URB submission.

`Ci:1:008:0` indicates that the URB is submitting a control request with an IN data stage (`Ci`) to bus 1, device `008`, endpoint `0`.

`s` indicates that the data that follows is the Setup stage's data.

`80 06 0100 0000 0012` is the Setup stage's data in hexadecimal.

`18` is the decimal number of bytes requested in the Data stage.

`<` terminates a log for the Setup stage of a control IN transfer.

Here is the device's response to the request:

```
dedeb680 223163748 C Ci:1:008:0 0 18 = 12010002 00000040 dc0513a8
      00300102 0301
```

`dedeb680` uses the same tag as the previous line because both lines have information about the same URB.

`223163748` is a timestamp in μs.

`C` indicates that the event is an URB callback.

`Ci:1:008:0` indicates that the URB submitted a control request with an IN data stage (`Ci`) to bus `1`, device `008`, endpoint `0`.

`0` is the URB's status (success). Error codes are in `/usr/include/asm/errno.h`. For USB-specific explanations of error codes returned from `usbcore`, see:

`kernel.org/doc/Documentation/usb/error-codes.txt`

`18` is the decimal number of bytes received in the Data stage.

`=` indicates that data follows.

`12010002 00000040 dc0513a8 00300102 0301` are the 18 hexadecimal bytes of the device descriptor returned by the device in the request's Data stage. (See Chapter 1 for an explanation of the device descriptor's contents.)

For more details and examples, see the Linux kernel documentation file `usbmon.txt`.

Decoding Text Logs with a Visual Display

If you're thinking that decoding usbmon's logs is a bit of a chore, an alternative is available. The `vusb-analyzer` application can decode and display usbmon's logs (Figure 4-1).

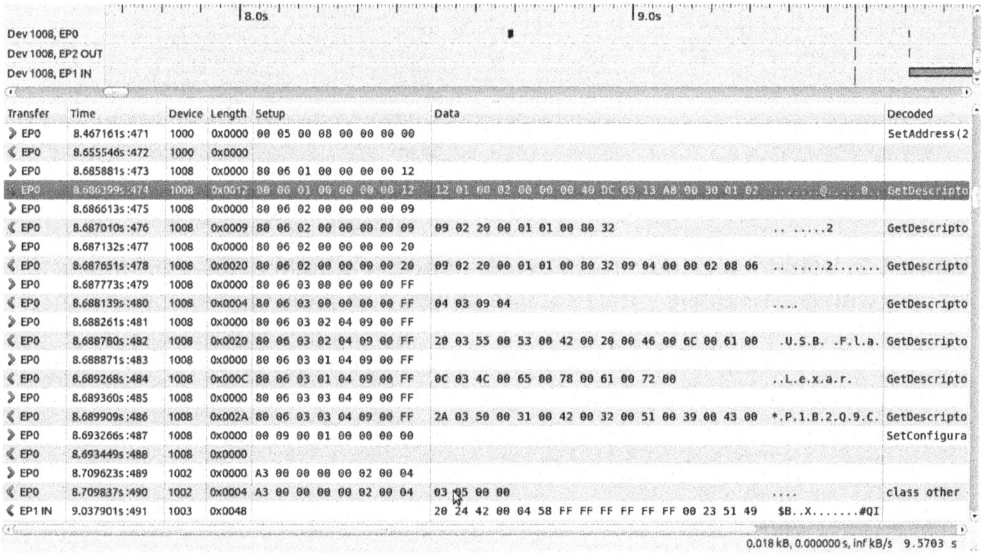

Figure 4-1. The vusb-analyzer utility decodes and displays usbmon log files.

The application, written in Python, is available from *vusb-analyzer.sourceforge.net*. The host system running vusb-analyzer must have Python and PyGTK bindings (py-gtk) installed. To see the graphical timeline, the system must have gnome-canvas and its Python bindings installed.

To view a log file, run the application, passing the log file's path and name as an argument. The file must have a .mon extension. This command, run from vusb-analzyer's directory, loads the file /home/jan/usbmon/usb1.mon:

./vusb-analyzer /home/jan/usbmon/usb1.mon

The main window's top pane is a timing diagram that shows when endpoint traffic occurred. The bottom pane displays the URBs. Each URB has two rows, one for when the driver submitted the URB (indicated by a right-pointing arrow) and one for when it completed (indicated by a left-pointing arrow).

The columns show the endpoint number and direction, time, device number, data length, contents of the Setup packet (present for endpoint zero only), the first 16 bytes of data, if present, in hexadecimal and ASCII, and any decoding performed such as the name of a control request.

To find out more about a transfer, double-click in its row. Figure 4-2 shows a request for the device descriptor:

```
0000: 12 01 00 02 00 00 00 40 DC 05 13 A8 00 30 01 02    .......@.....0..    GetDescriptor(0x00, 1)
0010: 03 01                                              ..
                                                                            device descriptor:
                                                                              bLength              = 18
                                                                              bDescriptorType      = 1
                                                                              bcdUSB               = 0x0200
                                                                              bDeviceClass         = 0x00
                                                                              bDeviceSubClass      = 0x00
                                                                              bDeviceProtocol      = 0x00
                                                                              bMaxPacketSize0      = 64
                                                                              idVendor             = 0x05DC
                                                                              idProduct            = 0xA813
                                                                              bcdDevice            = 0x3000
                                                                              iManufacturer        = 1
                                                                              iProduct             = 2
                                                                              iSerialNumber        = 3
                                                                              bNumConfigurations   = 1
```

Figure 4-2. Double-clicking a row in vusb-analyzer's main display brings up a window with more details. This example shows a request for a device

The left pane shows all of the data the device returned in hexadecimal and ASCII. The right pane decodes the data, showing the contents of the descriptor's fields.

As of version 1.1, vusb-analyzer doesn't decode class-specific traffic such as mass-storage request blocks, but the hexadecimal and ASCII displays provide a starting point for decoding.

5

Accessing Files on Drives

It's likely that the most popular USB devices for USB embedded host systems are flash drives. These drives are a solution when you need to store information in files, especially when you occasionally move files between an embedded system and another computer. A data logger can save data in files on a drive that you periodically attach to a PC to analyze. Or you can copy audio files to a drive on a PC and attach the drive to a portable player.

Inside the Mass Storage Class

Flash drives, hard drives, CDs, and DVDs belong to the USB mass-storage class. To access USB drives, the host must support the USB mass-storage class, SCSI commands, and the drive's file system.

The mass-storage class defines protocols for sending commands, data, and status information via USB. In a mass-storage device's interface descriptor, bInterfaceClass = 08h. Mass-storage communications use bulk transfers.

SCSI commands provide a framework for obtaining information about a storage device, controlling the device's operation, and reading and writing blocks of data in the storage media. Specifications for SCSI commands are available from the INCITS Technical Committee T10 (*t10.org*).

My book *USB Mass Storage* includes a guide to SCSI commands and other mass-storage protocols.

A file system defines a directory structure for storing file names and locations. Flash drives often use FAT32 for maximum compatibility with host OSes. Drives with capacities of less than 2 GB may use FAT16.

Mounting is the process of logically attaching a drive or a drive volume and making its file system accessible to software. The host's OS mounts a drive or volume to enable applications to access the drive or volume's files.

Embedded Host Support

Because flash drives are such popular devices, you're likely to find support for mass storage in any development platform with USB host support. The OS or other provided firmware typically manages mass-storage protocols and SCSI commands and supports one or more file systems. Firmware accesses mass-storage devices using functions, classes, or commands that create and read directories and open, read, write to, and close files.

Some flash drives are designed to work when attached to Windows systems but don't fully comply with the USB mass-storage specification. These drives often assume that the host will use the same sequence of commands that Windows uses. If you're developing low-level host firmware for mass storage, use a protocol analyzer to capture device communications with a Windows host to use as a model.

Preventing Data Loss due to Caching

To guard against losing data, applications that write to removable drives should be aware of the effects of caching. To improve overall system performance, instead of writing data immediately to a drive, a host may cache the data and write it to the drive after a large block of data has accumulated and the system isn't busy with other tasks. Several seconds may elapse between calling a function to write to a drive and the write operation that sends the cached data to the drive. If a user removes the drive before the write operation completes, the data is lost.

Disabling caching can reduce overall performance but also reduces the chance of losing data because a user removed a drive before the host had written all of the data to the drive. When caching is enabled, a `flush` or `sync` function can send data to the drive after each write operation.

Alternatives

SD Cards/MMCs are alternatives for removable devices that store information in files. With supporting firmware, a processor can access the cards via an SPI port or SD-Card bus. (USB host systems can access these cards by using a USB/SD-Card adapter.) An Ethernet or wireless network connection can also provide a way to exchange files with other systems.

Detecting a Drive

The example applications in this chapter use the include statements in Listing 5-1.

```
#include <mntent.h>
#include <stdio.h>
#include <stdlib.h>
#include <string.h>
#include <unistd.h
```

Listing 5-1: The mass-storage examples use these include statements.

To access files on a drive, a Linux application must know the file system's mount point. Firmware can search for any mounted drive or volume or select a drive or volume with a specific mount point.

About Mount Points

In Linux, a mount point is a virtual file that applications use to obtain access to files on a drive. Mounting associates a drive's or volume's device node with a mount point. Unmounting removes the association.

Chapter 4 introduced device nodes. The device node for the first drive that uses SCSI protocols is /dev/sda, with the device nodes for additional drives named sdb, sdc, and so on. A drive may have a different device node on each attachment depending on how many other drives the OS has already assigned device nodes for.

Most drives have a partition table that resides in the media's first sector and enables the drive to support multiple logical volumes. A drive with a partition table has a device node for each volume. For example, a drive with two volumes might have the device node /dev/sda for the drive plus /dev/sda1 and /dev/sda2 for the volumes. A drive without a partition table may have a single device node (/dev/sda).

The default directory that contains mount points for removable media is typically /media. The name of the default mount point is typically the volume label from the volume's root directory. For drives without volume labels, the default mount point is the volume's type with a numeric identifier if needed such as /media/disk, /media/disk-1, and so on.

You can obtain the mount point for a drive or partition by examining its mount descriptor in the /proc/mounts virtual file, which contains the mount point(s) and other information for each mounted device or volume.

This is an example mount descriptor for /dev/sda1 mounted at /media/Lexar:

```
/dev/sda1 /media/Lexar vfat rw,nosuid,nodev,relatime,uid=1000,gid=1000,
    fmask=0022,dmask=0077,codepage=cp437,iocharset=iso8859-1,
    shortname=mixed,showexec,utf8,flush,errors=remount-ro 0 0
```

The descriptor begins with the device node (/dev/sda1) followed by the mount point (/media/Lexar), the mounted file system (vfat), read/write access type (rw), a series of mount flags, and two dummy zeros. The descriptor ends with a line-feed code (0Ah).

Mounting and Unmounting a Drive

On attachment of a USB drive, the OS typically creates the mount point and mounts the drive. On removal, the OS unmounts the drive and deletes the mount point.

The udev rules introduced in Chapter 3 determines whether the OS mounts USB drives on attachment. For example, in /lib/udev/rules.d, an 80-udisks.rules file may set the UDISKS_PRESENTATION_NOPOLICY property to specify automounting (0) or no automounting (1) for specific devices or device types such as /dev/sd*. This rule specifies automouting for a variety of device types:

```
KERNEL=="sd*|hd*|sr*|mmcblk*|mspblk*", ENV{UDISKS_PRESENTATION_NOPOLICY}
    ="0"
```

When needed, the mount command can mount an unmounted drive or volume to an existing directory. These commands create the mount directory /media/mydrive and mount the volume at /dev/sda1 on the created directory:

```
sudo mkdir /media/mydrive
sudo mount /dev/sda1 /media/mydrive
```

The umount command (note just one "*n*" in umount!) unmounts a mounted drive or volume. This command unmounts the volume at /media/mydrive:

```
sudo umount /media/mydrive
```

Finding a Mount Point

To find a device's mount point, an application can search the /proc/mounts file. Listing 5-2 searches for an entry that contains "/dev/sda" and returns a pointer to the mount point or null if not found.

```
void get_mount_point(char *drive_mount_point, size_t max_length)
{
    char desired_mount_point[] = "dev/sda";
    struct mntent *mount_entry;
    FILE *fp = setmntent("/proc/mounts","r");
    memset(drive_mount_point, 0, max_length);

    do
    {
        mount_entry = getmntent(fp);
        if (mount_entry !=  NULL)
        {
            if (strstr(mount_entry->mnt_fsname, desired_mount_point)
                != NULL)
            {
                if (strlen(mount_entry->mnt_dir) < max_length)
                {
                    strncpy(drive_mount_point, mount_entry -> mnt_dir,
                        max_length);
                    printf("%s mounted on %s\n",mount_entry -> mnt_fsname,
                        drive_mount_point);
                }
                else
                {
                    printf("Error: mount point's path is too long.\n");
                }
            }
        }
    }
    while ((drive_mount_point[0] == 0) && (mount_entry != NULL));
}
```

Listing 5-2: This function searches the /proc/mounts file to find a drive's mount point.

The function accepts a pointer to a char array that will hold the retrieved mount point (drive_mount_point) and the length of the passed array (max_length). The array must be large enough to hold the mount point's complete path plus one byte for a null termination.

To find the mount point, the function uses the setmntent and getmntent functions and mntent structure defined in the GNU C library file mntent.h.

mount_entry is an mntent structure whose members correspond to the items in a mount descriptor. The mnt_fsname member holds a pointer to a string containing the device node for a mounted device or volume, such as /dev/sda or /dev/sda1. The mnt_dir member holds a pointer to a string containing the mount point of the device's file system, such as /media/Lexar.

A call to setmntent opens /proc/mounts for reading and returns a pointer to the file.

memset initializes the drive_mount_point array.

A do...while loop steps through the /proc/mounts entries searching for an entry containing "dev/sda".

A call to getmntent returns the next mntent structure in /proc/mounts or null if all entries have been retrieved. The strstr function searches the retrieved mnt_fsname elements for the text "dev/sda". For example, the element might contain /dev/sda or /dev/sda1. On finding a match, if the mount point will fit in the passed array, strncpy copies the mount point in mount_entry -> mnt_dir to the drive_mount_point array. The loop ends on finding on a match or on reaching the end of /proc/mounts without a match.

Checking if a Drive is Still Attached

After a program has detected a drive, if a user removes the drive, any attempt to read from a file on the drive will fail with an error on attempting to open the file. On device removal, if the mount point isn't deleted for some reason, a write operation to a detached drive can appear to succeed. Instead of writing to the drive, the write operation will write the data to a file associated with the drive's mount point. For example, if a drive's mount point was /media/mydrive, after detaching the drive, write operations may write data to a file at /media/mydrive instead of failing the operation.

To prevent writing to drives that are no longer attached, firmware can search for the drive's mount descriptor before each write to the drive. If the mount descriptor isn't present, the drive isn't mounted.

A small risk remains that a write to the drive will occur after a user has removed a drive but before the OS has removed the mount descriptor. Program code can monitor the mount descriptor and use an LED or other indicator to inform the user when it's safe to remove the drive, but this method still requires users to pay attention to the notification!

Listing 5-3 searches for a specific mount point and returns 1 if found and zero if not.

```c
int drive_available(char *drive_mount_point)
{
    int drive_available = 0;
    struct mntent *mount_entry;
    FILE *fp = setmntent("/proc/mounts","r");

    do
    {
        mount_entry = getmntent(fp);
        if (mount_entry !=  NULL)
        {
            drive_available = !(strcmp(mount_entry->mnt_dir,
                    drive_mount_point));
        }
    }
    while ((!drive_available) && (mount_entry != NULL));

    return drive_available;
}
```

Listing 5-3: This function searches /proc/mounts to find out if a specific drive is attached.

The function accepts a pointer to a null-terminated char array containing a mount point (drive_mount_point) returned by a call to the get_mount_point function above. As in the get_mount_point function, a do...while loop steps through the mount descriptors in /proc/mounts.

For each entry, the strcmp function searches for a match between the retrieved mount point (mount_entry->mnt_dir) and the desired mount point (drive_mount_point). The loop ends on finding a match or on reaching the end of the file without a match.

Reading and Writing to Files

The examples that follow use the routines above and demonstrate how to read and write to files on a drive.

Writing to a File

Listing 5-4 is an application that detects a USB drive, opens the file `my_data.txt` on the drive, appends a string to the file's contents, and closes the file.

```c
int drive_available(char* drive_mount_point);
void get_mount_point(char *drive_mount_point, size_t max_length);

int main()
{
    #define MAX_PATH_LENGTH 255

    char *file_name_and_path = "my_data.txt";
    FILE *fp = NULL;
    char mount_point_and_file[MAX_PATH_LENGTH] = {0};
    int drive_mount_point_max_length = MAX_PATH_LENGTH
        -strlen(file_name_and_path) - 1;

    char drive_mount_point[drive_mount_point_max_length];

    memset(drive_mount_point, 0, drive_mount_point_max_length);

    get_mount_point(drive_mount_point, sizeof(drive_mount_point));

    if (drive_mount_point != NULL)
    {
        strncpy(mount_point_and_file, drive_mount_point,
          sizeof(drive_mount_point));
        strcat(mount_point_and_file, "/");
        strcat(mount_point_and_file, file_name_and_path);

        char *write_buffer = "Mass storage write test.\r\n";

        if (drive_available(drive_mount_point))
        {
            fp = fopen(mount_point_and_file, "a");
```

Listing 5-4: This application writes data to a file on a drive. (Part 1 of 2)

```
            if (fp != NULL)
            {
                if (fwrite(write_buffer, strlen(write_buffer), 1, fp) > 0)
                {
                    fclose(fp);
                    sync();
                    printf("Data written to the file.\n");
                }
                else
                {
                    printf("Write failed. Zero bytes written to the file.\n");
                }
            }
            else
            {
                printf("Write failed. Error opening the file.\n");
            }
        }
        else
        {
            printf("Write failed. Drive attached?\n");
        }
    }
    else
    {
        printf("Write failed. Drive attached?\n");
    }

    return 0;
}
```

Listing 5-4: This application writes data to a file on a drive. (Part 2 of 2)

The application uses the get_mount_point and drive_available functions above in this chapter.

The application identifies the file by its complete path, which consists of the drive's mount point, the file's path on the drive, and the filename. MAX_PATH_LENGTH is the maximum length of the mount point plus the path to the file on the drive and the filename.

The size of `drive_mount_point` is set to `MAX_PATH_LENGTH` minus the length of the file name and path on the drive and one character for a "/" separator between the mount point and the file name and path.

memset initializes the `drive_mount_point` array.

A call to `get_mount_point` attempts to retrieve a mount point for the drive. On success, `strncpy` copies the mount point to the `mount_point_and_file` array, and `strcat` adds the "/" separator and the file name and path to the string.

`write_buffer` contains the data to write to the file.

A call to `drive_available` verifies that the drive is still attached. On success, `fopen` opens the file specified in `mount_point_and_file` for appending and returns a pointer to the file. If the file doesn't exist, `fopen` creates the file.

On opening the file, `fwrite` accepts a buffer of data to write, the number of units to write, the size of the units in bytes, and the retrieved file pointer. The function returns the number of bytes written.

`fclose` sends the buffered data to the file's output stream for writing to the drive and closes the file.

`sync` sends any unsent buffered data to the drive.

Reading from a File

Listing 5-5 is an application that detects a USB drive, opens the file `config.txt` on the drive, reads data from the file, searches the data for defined commands, and turns LEDs on or off according to the commands read from the file.

```
#include "led_control.h"

void get_mount_point(char* drive_mount_point, size_t max_length);
void led_control(int led_number, int led_state);
void led_initialize();

int main()
{
    #define MAX_READ_LENGTH 20
    #define MAX_PATH_LENGTH 255
```

Listing 5-5: This application reads data from a file and takes action according to the data read. (Part 1 of 3)

```
char buffer[MAX_READ_LENGTH + 1] = {0};
int chars_read = 0;
char *file_name_and_path = "config.txt";
char mount_point_and_file[MAX_PATH_LENGTH] = {0};
int drive_mount_point_max_length = MAX_PATH_LENGTH -
      strlen(file_name_and_path) - 1;
char drive_mount_point[drive_mount_point_max_length];

memset(drive_mount_point, 0, drive_mount_point_max_length);
led_initialize();
FILE *fp = setmntent("/proc/mounts","r");
get_mount_point(drive_mount_point, sizeof(drive_mount_point));
if (drive_mount_point != NULL)
{
   strncpy(mount_point_and_file, drive_mount_point,
       sizeof(drive_mount_point));
   strcat(mount_point_and_file, "/");
   strcat(mount_point_and_file, file_name_and_path);
   fp = fopen(mount_point_and_file, "r");

   if (fp != NULL)
   {
      chars_read = fread (buffer, 1, MAX_READ_LENGTH, fp);
      fclose(fp);

      if (chars_read)
      {
         if (strstr(buffer, "led1on") != NULL)
         {
            led_control(0, 1);
            printf("led1on\n");
         }
```

Listing 5-5: This application reads data from a file and takes action according to the data read. (Part 2 of 3)

```
            if (strstr(buffer, "led1off") != NULL)
            {
               led_control(0, 0);
               printf("led1off\n");
            }
            if (strstr(buffer, "led2on") != NULL)
            {
               led_control(1, 1);
               printf("led2on\n");
            }
            if (strstr(buffer, "led2off") != NULL)
            {
               led_control(1, 0);
               printf("led2off\n");
            }
         }
         else
         {
            printf("Zero bytes read from the file.\n");
         }
      }
      else
      {
         printf("Error opening the file.\n");
      }
   }
   return 0;
}
```

Listing 5-5: This application reads data from a file and takes action according to the data read. (Part 3 of 3)

The defined commands are led1on, led1off, led2on, and led2off.

The application calls the led_initialize and led_control functions from Chapter 3. To enable controlling the LEDs, run the application with sudo or create a udev rule as described in Chapter 3. The application also uses the get_mount_point function presented earlier in this chapter.

MAX_READ_LENGTH is the maximum number of characters the application will attempt to read from a file. The values for MAX_PATH_LENGTH, file_name_and_path, mount_point_and_file, drive_mount_point_max_length, and drive_mount_point have the same uses as in the previous example.

As in the previous example, a call to get_mount_point attempts to retrieve a mount point for the drive. On success, strncpy and strcat store the mount point and file name in the mount_point_and_file array.

fopen opens the specified file on the drive for reading and returns a pointer to the file.

If the file opens, fread reads up to MAX_READ_LENGTH characters from the file into a buffer and fclose closes the file.

The strstr function searches for defined commands in the data read. On finding a defined command, a call to led_control turns the specified LED on or off.

To test the application, create the file config.txt and store these two lines of text in the file:

led1on

led2off

Save the file to a flash drive and attach the drive to the host system.

After testing with this file, you can change the commands in the file and retest.

6

Getting User Input

The human interface device (HID) class encompasses user-input devices such as keyboards and keypads, mice, and game controllers. Many barcode readers are HIDs that function as USB keyboards with the barcode data emulating keypresses. Other HIDs include uninterruptible power supply (UPS) units, on-screen control panels for display monitors, and devices with vendor-defined functions.

Inside the Human Interface Device Class

In a HID's interface descriptor, bInterfaceClass = 03h. HIDs use control and interrupt transfers.

Embedded Host Support

Some USB host development platforms provide drivers for accessing USB keyboards and mice. Built-in support for other HID functions, including vendor-specific functions, is less common. Chapter 10 shows how a Linux application can access HIDs with vendor-specific functions.

Using HID Reports

All HID data travels in reports, which are data structures defined by the HID's report descriptor. All HIDs must support Input reports, which carry data from the device to the host. HIDs may also support Output reports, which carry data from the host to the device, and Feature reports, which can travel in either direction. Input and Output reports can use interrupt or control transfers. Feature reports always use control transfers. A HID can support one or more reports of each type.

Every HID has a class-specific report descriptor that defines the HID's reports. Listing 6-1 shows a report descriptor for a keyboard.

In the report descriptor, Usage codes provide information about how to interpret the report data. For example, Usage codes tell the host that the first byte in a system keyboard's report indicates whether any Shift, Control, or GUI keys are pressed.

The host requests a report descriptor by sending a Get_Descriptor control request to the HID interface. In the Setup packet's wValue field, the high byte = 22h to request a report descriptor.

Generic Desktop Controls

The HID class defines Generic Desktop controls as system devices such as keyboards, mice, and game controllers. Report descriptors for these devices contain the Usage Page code for Generic Desktop (0501h) followed by a Usage ID for a keyboard (0906h), mouse (0902h), or other Generic Desktop control.

To find a system keyboard or other Generic Desktop control, a host can search the report descriptors of attached HIDs for the codes that indicate the desired function. A host can also identify a specific HID by the Vendor ID and Product ID in the device descriptor.

Keyboard Reports

System keyboards typically send 8-byte Input reports. Byte zero is a bitmap that indicates if any Control, Shift, Alt, or GUI keys are pressed. Byte 1 is reserved. Bytes 2–7 can identify up to six keys pressed at once. The USB-IF's *HID Usage Tables* document defines the key codes, which are not the same as ASCII character codes. For example, the code for "a" is 04h, and in report byte zero, if the second bit (indicating the left shift key) or sixth bit (the right shift key) = 1, the letter is upper case.

Pressing only the "A" key results in this report:

00h 00h 04h 00h 00h 00h 00h 00h

Pressing Left Shift and "A" results in this report:

02h 00h 04h 00h 00h 00h 00h 00h

GetDescriptor (Report)

HID Report Descriptor	
Item	**Data**
Usage Page *(Generic Desktop)*	05 01
Usage *(Keyboard)*	09 06
Collection *(Application)*	A1 01
Usage Page *(Keyboard)*	05 07
Usage Minimum *(Keyboard Left Control)*	19 E0
Usage Maximum *(Keyboard Right GUI)*	29 E7
Logical minimum *(0)*	15 00
Logical maximum *(1)*	25 01
Report Size *(1)*	75 01
Report Count *(8)*	95 08
Input *(Data,Value,Absolute,Bit Field)*	81 02
Report Count *(1)*	95 01
Report Size *(8)*	75 08
Input *(Constant,Array,Absolute,Bit Field)*	81 01
Report Count *(3)*	95 03
Report Size *(1)*	75 01
Usage Page *(LEDs)*	05 08
Usage Minimum *(Num Lock)*	19 01
Usage Maximum *(Scroll Lock)*	29 03
Output *(Data,Value,Absolute,Non-volatile,Bit Field)*	91 02
Report Count *(5)*	95 05
Report Size *(1)*	75 01
Output *(Constant,Array,Absolute,Non-volatile,Bit Field)*	91 01
Report Count *(6)*	95 06
Report Size *(8)*	75 08
Logical minimum *(0)*	15 00
Logical maximum *(255)*	26 FF 00
Usage Page *(Keyboard)*	05 07
Usage Minimum *(No event indicated)*	19 00
⚓ Usage Maximum *(Unknown (0x00FF))*	2A FF 00
Input *(Data,Array,Absolute,Bit Field)*	81 00
End Collection	C0

Listing 6-1: This display from an Ellisys protocol analyzer shows a keyboard's report descriptor. (Part 1 of 2)

Input Report 0		
Bit offset	Bit count	Description
0	1	Keyboard Left Control
1	1	Keyboard Left Shift
2	1	Keyboard Left Alt
3	1	Keyboard Left GUI
4	1	Keyboard Right Control
5	1	Keyboard Right Shift
6	1	Keyboard Right Alt
7	1	Keyboard Right GUI
8	8	(Not used)
16	8	Keyboard Array
24	8	Keyboard Array
32	8	Keyboard Array
40	8	Keyboard Array
48	8	Keyboard Array
56	8	Keyboard Array

Output Report 0		
Bit offset	Bit count	Description
0	1	Num Lock
1	1	Caps Lock
2	1	Scroll Lock
3	1	(Not used)
4	1	(Not used)
5	1	(Not used)
6	1	(Not used)
7	1	(Not used)

Listing 6-1: This display from an Ellisys protocol analyzer shows a keyboard's report descriptor. (Part 2 of 2)

A system keyboard may also accept 1-byte Output reports whose first three bits tell the device how to set the Num Lock, Caps Lock, and Scroll Lock LEDs.

Mouse Reports

System mice typically send reports with three bits that indicate the states of three buttons followed by 5 pad bits and two bytes that indicate x-axis and y-axis movement.

The USB-IF's *Device Class Definition for Human Interface Devices (HID)* includes an example report descriptor for a mouse.

Composite Devices

Many keyboards are composite devices that include a second interface for a pointing device such as a touchpad. Even when the keyboard doesn't have a physical pointing device, the device may return descriptors for the function. Host firmware that supports keyboards should take care to examine the Usage codes for each interface to find the keyboard's interface.

Alternatives

Embedded systems have several options besides USB for receiving user input. A touch screen provides user input and a display in a single unit and can emulate a full keyboard or a custom keypad. Touch screens typically use a dedicated 4- or 5-line interface. Devices that need only a few inputs can use buttons or switches wired to general-purpose input pins.

The legacy interfaces for keyboards, mice, and game controllers are another option if suitable hardware is available. The legacy interfaces are PS/2 for keyboards, PS/2 and serial for mice, and the analog game-port interface.

Reading Keypresses

On a conventional PC, the keyboard is one of the fundamental ways for users to interact with the computer. Embedded systems tend to require less user input, but an embedded system might use a keyboard or keypad for data entry or to enable users to select functions, actions, or configuration options.

Using Standard Input Devices

On Linux and other OSes, the command line accepts input from standard input devices, which include system keyboards. When you run an application from a command line in Linux, the application can use functions defined in the GNU C library file `stdio.h` to read input from standard input devices such as keyboards . The companion to standard input is standard output. Applications write standard output to the display screen or other standard output device.

Reading Keyboard Input

The applications below use keyboard input to control an LED. The applications call the `led_initialize` and `led_control` functions from Chapter 3. To enable controlling the LEDs, run the application with sudo or create a udev rule as described in Chapter 3.

Listing 6-2 reads input that terminates in the newline character that results when the user presses **Enter**. The input can come from a keyboard or a device such as a barcode scanner that emulates a keyboard. The example uses keypresses to control an LED, but an application can use keypress input in any way. For example, a routine could read a scanned barcode and retrieve product information that corresponds to the barcode.

```c
#include <stdio.h>
#include "led_control.h"
void led_initialize();

int main()
{
   int keypress;

   led_initialize();

   printf("Keyboard read demo.\n");
   printf("To turn on the usr0 LED, press 1, then Enter.\n");
   printf("To turn off the usr0 LED, press 0, then Enter.\n");
   printf("Press Ctrl+C to end the program.\n");
   for (;;)
   {
      keypress = fgetc(stdin);
      if (keypress == '0')
      {
         printf("The usr0 LED is off.\n");
         led_control(0, 0);
      }
```

Listing 6-2: This application reads keypresses from a keyboard. (Part 1 of 2)

```
        else if (keypress == '1')
        {
            printf("The usr0 LED is on.\n");
            led_control(0, 1);
        }
    }
    return 0;
}
```

Listing 6-2: This application reads keypresses from a keyboard. (Part 2 of 2)

In the application, an endless `for` loop calls the `stdin` function `fgetc`, which waits for keyboard input that terminates in the newline character.

On receiving a newline character, `fgetc` sequentially returns any keypresses that preceded the newline. If the user pressed "0", the application calls a function to turn off the LED. If the user pressed "1", the application calls a function to turn on the LED. The application ignores other keypresses except `Ctrl+C`, which ends the application.

Reading Keyboard Input without Blocking

In the example above, the application waits for the newline code that indicates the end of an input string. Most systems have other things to do besides waiting for keypresses. To enable performing other tasks while waiting for input, an application can create a thread or process that waits for keypresses and signals the application when input is available.

Another way to read input without blocking is to use the `ncurses` library. To use `ncurses`, your toolchain must include the `libncurses` library compiled for your target architecture. The Ångström toolchain includes this library. To compile an application that uses functions in the `ncurses` library, use the `-lncurses` switch.

Listing 6-3's application uses the `ncurses` library.

```
#include <ncurses.h>
#include <signal.h>
#include <stdio.h>
#include <stdlib.h>
#include <string.h>
#include "led_control.h"
```

Listing 6-3: The ncurses library enables reading the keyboard without blocking. (Part 1 of 3)

```
void led_initialize();
void sigint_handler(int sig);

int main()
{
    int keypress;

    led_initialize();
    initscr();
    signal (SIGINT, (void*) sigint_handler);

    printw("Keyboard read demo.\n");
    printw("Press 1 to turn on usr0. Press 0 to turn off usr0\n");
    printw("Press Ctrl+C to end the program.\n");

    nodelay(stdscr, TRUE);

    for (;;)
    {
        keypress = getch();
        if (keypress == '0')
        {
            led_control(0, 0);
        }
        if (keypress == '1')
        {
            led_control(0, 1);
        }
    }
    sleep(1);
    return 0;
}
```

Listing 6-3: The ncurses library enables reading the keyboard without blocking.
(Part 2 of 3)

```
void  sigint_handler(int sig)
{
   endwin();
   exit (sig);
}
```

Listing 6-3: The ncurses library enables reading the keyboard without blocking. (Part 3 of 3)

In the application, an endless loop checks for keypresses and can perform other tasks when the keyboard is idle. This approach can be useful when a system needs to respond to occasional user input such as a request to start or stop collecting data. The delay in responding to keypresses depends on the amount of time the system spends on other tasks in the loop.

A call to initscr enables using ncurses functions for keyboard input.

The GNU C library's signal function assigns a handler to reset the terminal when the user ends the application. SIGINT represents the key combination that interrupts the application (Ctrl+C). The handler is the sigint_handler routine.

printw is the ncurses replacement for printf.

nodelay configures getch as non-blocking (TRUE) on the default terminal window represented by stdscr.

An endless for loop reads keypress data and can perform other tasks.

getch returns the value of the keypress or ERR if no key was pressed. The led_control functions turn an LED on or off in response to a keypress of "0" or "1". Pressing Ctrl+C ends the application.

sleep is a placeholder representing other tasks the application may perform.

When the program ends, sigint_handler calls the ncurses function endwin to reset the terminal and exit to terminate the program.

7

Bridging to Other Interfaces

USB devices can function as bridges, or adapters, for communicating on other interfaces. The USB communications devices class defines protocols for using USB as a bridge to phone systems, Ethernet networks, and USB virtual COM ports. The USB wireless controller class defines protocols for communicating over Bluetooth. Vendor-specific drivers can enable communicating with devices that function as bridges to wireless networks and other interfaces.

Inside the Communications Devices Class

A device in the communications devices class (CDC) can declare the class in both the device descriptor (bDeviceClass = 02h) and an interface descriptor (bInterfaceClass = 02h) or in an interface descriptor only. In either case, in the CDC interface, bInterfaceSubclass names a communications model, or function, and bInterfaceProtocol names a CDC protocol if needed.

CDC devices typically use bulk transfers for data.

Embedded Host Support

Some USB embedded host modules, OSes, and other firmware support communicating via USB virtual serial ports in the communications devices class. Built-in support for other CDC functions is less common. Linux drivers are available for the class's major functions.

Devices That Use Vendor-specific Drivers

Some devices that perform CDC-supported functions use vendor-specific drivers instead of the CDC driver. To access these devices, the host system must provide a compatible driver for the device.

For example, many USB virtual-serial-port devices, including most commercial USB/serial adapters, contain controller chips that use vendor-specific protocols and thus use vendor-specific drivers on the host. These devices have become popular because they have better performance and enhanced capabilities compared to devices that use the CDC driver included with Windows. Sources for the controllers include FTDI, MosChip Semiconductor Technology Ltd., Prolific Technology Inc., and Silicon Laboratories.

Applications access serial ports in much the same way whether accessing a physical serial port, a CDC USB virtual serial port, or a USB virtual serial port with a vendor-specific driver. The hardware-specific protocols are handled at a lower level.

In a similar way, some USB/Ethernet bridges use vendor-specific protocols and drivers instead of USB CDC drivers. USB/wireless-network bridges don't have a defined class and must use vendor-specific drivers. Applications that use high-level network protocols such as TCP/IP access the network in the same way whether accessing a physical Ethernet port, a CDC USB/Ethernet bridge, or a wired or wireless network bridge with a vendor-specific driver.

Linux drivers are available for popular devices that perform CDC functions using vendor-defined protocols.

Alternatives

Embedded systems that have physical ports for serial, Ethernet, wireless-network, and Bluetooth communications don't need USB bridges to communicate on these interfaces. However, USB provides a way to support one or more ports that users can add or remove as needed.

Using a USB Virtual Serial Port

USB virtual-serial-port devices are popular because they can transfer data for vendor-defined purposes and because they support the familiar serial-port programming interface. A device with a virtual serial port can use the data in any way. In fact, the device doesn't have to have an asynchronous serial port at all. For example, FTDI's FT245x USB FIFO chip can appear as a serial port to the host but functions as a USB/parallel converter.

Virtual serial-port devices in the CDC class use bInterfaceSubclass = 02h (abstract control model). For compatibility with host drivers, the interface descriptor typically sets bInterfaceProtocol = 01h (AT commands protocol), even if the device doesn't use AT commands. In the Linux application below, the only USB-specific code is the line that names the port to open. The first USB virtual serial port is at /dev/ttyUSB0, while the first physical serial port is at /dev/tty0. Everything else is identical to communicating with a physical serial port.

The Application

The example application waits to receive commands on the serial port and on detecting a defined command, takes action. The remote computer that sends commands can be a PC or other computer with terminal-emulator software and a built-in serial port or a USB/serial-port adapter. Use a null-modem cable or adapter if needed to route each serial port's TX output to the other serial port's RX input. At the remote computer, set up the terminal-emulator software to match the settings in the local system. The example uses 115,200 bps and no flow control for the serial ports.

From the remote computer, the user types commands followed by **Enter**. The embedded host searches the received data for defined commands and on finding one, turns an LED on or off. The application opens the port, gets and examines data received by the port, writes data to the port, and on closing the application, closes the port. Listing 7-1 shows the application's include statements, function prototypes, defines, and application-level variables.

```
#include <fcntl.h>
#include <signal.h>
#include <stdlib.h>
#include <termios.h>
#include "led_control.h"
```

Listing 7-1: The virtual serial port application uses these include statements, definitions, and variables. (Part 1 of 2)

```
void respond_to_command(char *read_buffer, int chars_read);
void serial_port_close();
void serial_port_open(void);
int serial_port_read(char *read_buffer, size_t max_chars_to_read);
void serial_port_write(char *write_buffer);
void sigint_handler(int sig);

#define MAX_COMMAND_LENGTH 10
static const char *PORT_NAME = "/dev/ttyUSB0";

int serial_port;
struct termios options_original;
```

Listing 7-1: The virtual serial port application uses these include statements, definitions, and variables. (Part 2 of 2)

The application calls the led_initialize and led_control functions from Chapter 3. To enable controlling the LEDs, run the application with sudo or create a udev rule as described in Chapter 3.

Listing 7-2 is the application's main function:

```
int main()
{
   int chars_read;
   char read_buffer[MAX_COMMAND_LENGTH + 1] = {0};

   led_initialize();
   serial_port_open();

   if (serial_port != -1)
   {
      signal (SIGINT, (void*)sigint_handler);

      serial_port_write("USB virtual serial port test program\r\n");
      serial_port_write("To control the usr0 LED, type led1on or led1off
        and press <Enter>\r\n");
      serial_port_write("To end the remote application, type closeapp
        and press <Enter> \r\n");
```

Listing 7-2: This application uses a virtual serial port to communicate with a remote system. (Part 1 of 2)

```
      printf("Waiting to receive commands...\n");
   }
   printf("Press Ctrl+C to exit the program.\n");

   for (;;)
   {
      if (serial_port != -1)
      {
         chars_read = serial_port_read(read_buffer, MAX_COMMAND_LENGTH);
         if (chars_read > 0)
         {
            respond_to_command(read_buffer, chars_read);
         }
      }
      // The application can perform other tasks here.
   }
   return 0;
}
```

Listing 7-2: This application uses a virtual serial port to communicate with a remote system. (Part 2 of 2)

The function initializes the LEDs (see Chapter 3) and calls a series of functions defined below in this chapter.

read_buffer is a char array that can hold MAX_COMMAND_LENGTH bytes plus a null termination.

The serial_port_open function opens the serial port. On success, a call to the GNU C library's signal function assigns the sigint_handler function to execute on Ctrl+C. Calls to the serial_port_write function send a series of messages to the serial port. An endless for loop then attempts to read data from the port.

The serial_port_read function returns up to MAX_COMMAND_LENGTH bytes into the read_buffer array.

On receiving data, a call to the respond_to_command function passes a pointer to the buffer and the number of characters read. The function searches the received data for defined commands and takes action as appropriate.

When not responding to commands, the application can perform other tasks. The application ends when the local user presses Ctrl+C or the remote computer sends a closeapp command.

Open the Port

Listing 7-3's function opens the USB virtual serial port.

```
void serial_port_open(void)
{
   struct termios options;
   serial_port = open(PORT_NAME, O_RDWR | O_NONBLOCK);

   if (serial_port != -1)
   {
      printf("Serial Port open\n");
      tcgetattr(serial_port,&options_original);
      tcgetattr(serial_port, &options);
      cfsetispeed(&options, B115200);
      cfsetospeed(&options, B115200);
      options.c_cflag |= (CLOCAL | CREAD);
      options.c_lflag |= ICANON;
      tcsetattr(serial_port, TCSANOW, &options);
   }
   else
      printf("Unable to open /dev/ttyUSB0\n");
}
```

Listing 7-3: This function opens a virtual serial port for communications.

The open function opens the port at /dev/ttyUSB0 and returns the port's file descriptor or -1 on error. The O_RDWR parameter opens the port for reading and writing, and O_NONBLOCK causes read operations to return immediately even if no data is available for reading.

Functions defined in the GNU C library file termios.h enable saving and restoring the terminal-emulator application's attributes. If the port opens, the termios function tcgetatt saves the terminal's attributes in two locations. The options_original structure saves the options for restoring when the application ends. The options structure holds the options the application will use.

Some of the terminal options apply only if the device functions as a bridge to an asynchronous serial port. For example, cfsetispeed and cfsetospeed set the baud rate for asynchronous serial receive and transmit, and CLOCAL causes the terminal to ignore modem control lines. Virtual serial ports that don't function as bridges to asynchronous serial ports don't use these options.

The CREAD parameter enables the receiver. ICANON buffers data by lines so received data is available only after receiving the newline character that results when the user presses **Enter**.

A call to tcsetattr implements the options for the terminal.

Read from the Port

Listing 7-4's function attempts to read from the serial port and returns the number of bytes read.

```
int serial_port_read(char *read_buffer, size_t max_chars_to_read)
{
    int chars_read = read(serial_port, read_buffer, max_chars_to_read);

    return chars_read;
}
```

Listing 7-4: The read function reads data from the virtual serial port.

The function accepts a pointer to a buffer that will hold the data (read_buffer) and the maximum number of characters to read into the buffer (max_chars_to_read), which should be no greater than the buffer's length. The read function attempts to read up to the specified number of characters from the port and returns the number of bytes read, which may be zero.

Write to the Port

Listing 7-5's function writes data to a serial port.

```
void serial_port_write(char *write_buffer)
{
    int bytes_written;
    size_t len = 0;

    len = strlen(write_buffer);
    bytes_written = write(serial_port, write_buffer, len);
    if (bytes_written < len)
    {
        printf("Write failed. \r\n");
    }
}
```

Listing 7-5: The write function writes data to a virtual serial port.

The function accepts a pointer to a buffer that contains a null-terminated string of data to write (write_buffer). The write function writes the data in write_buffer to the port and returns the number of bytes written.

Close the Port

Listing 7-6's function restores the saved options in options_original and closes the serial port.

```
void serial_port_close()
{
   tcsetattr(serial_port,TCSANOW,&options_original);
   close(serial_port);
}
```

Listing 7-6: The close function closes the virtual serial port.

Examine Received Data

Listing 7-7's function looks for defined commands and takes action as appropriate.

```
void respond_to_command(char *read_buffer, int chars_read)
{
   if (strstr(read_buffer, "led1on") != NULL)
   {
      led_control(0, 1);
      serial_port_write("led1 is on\r\n");
   }
   else if (strstr(read_buffer, "led1off") != NULL)
   {
      led_control(0, 0);
      serial_port_write("led1 is off\r\n");
   }
   else if (strstr(read_buffer, "closeapp") != NULL)
   {
      serial_port_close();
      exit(EXIT_SUCCESS);
   }
```

Listing 7-7: String functions search for defined commands in the received data. (Part 1 of 2)

```
else
{
   // Ignore undefined commands.
}
}
```

Listing 7-7: String functions search for defined commands in the received data. (Part 2 of 2)

The function accepts a pointer to a buffer containing a null-terminated string of received data and the number of characters received. The `strstr` function searches the string for a defined command.

If the array contains "`led1on`" or "`led1off`", the function turns an LED on or off as specified and writes a message to the serial port. If the buffer contains "`closeapp`", the function calls `serial_port_close` and exits the application.

Handle Ctrl + C

Listing 7-8's function executes when the user presses `Ctrl+C`.

```
void  sigint_handler(int sig)
{
   serial_port_close();
   exit (sig);
}
```

Listing 7-8: This function executes when the user presses Ctrl+C.

The function calls the `serial_port_close` function and exits the program.

Communicating on a Network

With a USB/Ethernet or USB/wireless-network adapter, a system can access local networks and gain access to the Internet.

Wired and Wireless Options

For wired networks, the USB communications devices class defines two subclasses that support Ethernet communications, the Ethernet control model (ECM) and the Ethernet emulation model (EEM). A USB/Ethernet adapter may use either CDC subclass or a vendor-defined protocol. USB/wireless-network adapters use vendor-defined protocols and drivers. All of the adapters use bulk transfers for network traffic.

Linux drivers are available for many wired and wireless network adapters.

Connecting

Linux systems have a variety of options available for managing network connections. In fact, one issue in setting up networking is making sure multiple tools aren't fighting to control the connection. In Ubuntu's Unity Desktop, view network settings from **System Settings > System > Network Tools**.

The NetworkManager tools (*live.gnome.org/NetworkManager*) can manage network configurations and automatically join previously detected networks. In Ubuntu, view and configure NetworkManager's settings from **System Settings > Internet and Network > Network Connections**.

Another popular network manager is wicd. Instead of using a network manager, you can configure network settings in the /etc/network/interfaces file as described below. Whatever tool you choose, be aware that you may need to disable or completely remove competing tools to enable using your chosen tool.

Static and Dynamic IP Addresses

To communicate on a network that uses Internet protocols, a system must have an IP address. A system can request an IP address from a DHCP server on the network or declare a static, or fixed, IP address. On the BeagleBoard-xM, a static IP address overcomes a driver limitation that otherwise causes the DHCP server to assign a different IP address to the USB/Ethernet port on each bootup.

DHCP servers typically keep a record of assigned IP addresses and the corresponding MAC addresses of the Ethernet ports. On detecting a previously used MAC address, the DHCP server assigns the IP address from the record. Ethernet controllers typically have fixed MAC addresses so the IP address remains the same between bootups.

The BeagleBoard-xM's driver for the LAN9514 Ethernet controller assigns a different, random MAC address to the Ethernet controller on each bootup. The new MAC address causes the DHCP server to assign a new IP address. Assigning a static IP address keeps the IP address from changing even if the MAC address changes.

In the **Network Connections** interface, you can edit a connection's settings to specify a static IP address. However, due to a bug with this feature, many systems configure static IP addresses in the /etc/network/interfaces file instead. NetworkManager should ignore any connection listed in /etc/network/interfaces.

Listing 7-9 shows an entry in `/etc/network/interfaces` that configures USB/Ethernet adapter `usb0` to use a static IP address.

```
auto usb0
iface usb0 inet static
    address 192.168.1.83
    netmask 255.255.255.0
    network 192.168.1.0
    gateway 192.168.1.254
```

Listing 7-9: The /etc/network/interfaces file can configure network settings.

`auto usb0` causes the `ifup -a` command, typically found in boot scripts, to bring up the `usb0` interface.

`iface usb0 inet static` introduces a *stanza* that describes the `usb0` interface. The `inet` option indicates that the interface uses TCP/IP. The `static` option indicates that the interface uses a static IP address.

`address` is the port's IP address. The address must be within the local network as described below.

`netmask` and `network` together define the local network. In the example, addresses from 192.168.1.0 to 192.168.1.255 are in the local network.

`gateway` is the address to use when forwarding traffic to IP addresses outside the local network.

To find what values to use for an existing network, from a command line on a Linux PC in the local network, enter `netstat -nr` to view the kernel IP routing table:

```
Kernel IP routing table
Destination  Gateway        Genmask        Flags  MSS  Window  irtt  Iface
192.168.1.0  0.0.0.0        255.255.255.0  U      0    0       0     usb0
0.0.0.0      192.168.1.254  0.0.0.0        UG     0    0       0     usb0
```

In the first row of data, `Destination` (192.168.1.0) is the network value, and `Genmask` (255.255.255.0) is the netmask.

In the bottom row, `Gateway` (192.168.1.254) is the gateway value. Under `Flags`, `U` means the route is up and `G` means the entry is the path for routing traffic outside the local network.

For more about the interfaces file, see the man page for `interfaces`.

Wireless Networks and Security

Wireless networks are especially useful for portable systems that don't stay in one place. Many wireless networks use security protocols to limit access and encrypt the network traffic. In the wireless router's configuration, the network administrator specifies the network's name, or service set ID (SSID), and the security protocol and password if used. Wireless security protocols include WPA and WPA2.

To access a secured network, the system must know the desired network's name, the security protocol, and the network password, or key. The **Network Tools** window shows the names of any detected networks and can store a security method and password for a wireless network. In the **Wireless** tab, select the desired network. Click **Edit**, and in the **Wireless Security** tab, select a **Security** type and enter the password.

You can view a wireless network's password from **Network Connections** in another Linux system in the network. From the network's **Wireless Security** tab, check the **Show password** box to reveal the password.

Systems that don't use a network manager can provide a `wpa_supplicant.conf` file with names of wireless networks and their WPA security policies and passwords. The `wpa_supplicant` program uses the information in the file to log into wireless networks. For an example file, see the documentation for `wpasupplicant` in `/usr/share/doc/wpasupplicant`.

Decoding URLs

To access URLs such as *janaxelson.com*, the system needs access to a domain name server (DNS) that can match URLs to their IP addresses. Linux uses the DNS addresses stored in the `/etc/resolv.conf` file. Note no "e" after "v" in resolv.conf!

You can add your server's address to `/etc/resolv.conf`:

```
nameserver 192.168.1.254
```

If you don't know the nameserver's IP address, view `/etc/resolv.conf` in another Linux system on the network. Or to view the addresses on a Windows system in the network, click **Start, Run**, enter `cmd`, and in the window that appears, enter `ipconfig /all`.

Exchanging Data

Applications don't have to know or care whether a network has a USB/Ethernet or USB/wireless-network adapter or a physical Ethernet or wireless-network ports. The hardware-specific details are handled at a lower lever.

The `scp` command can transfer files within a local network:

```
scp helloworld jan@192.168.1.83:/home/jan/my_data/
```

The command above transfers a file in the current directory (`helloworld`) to a destination specified by user (`jan`), IP address (`192.168.1.83`), and directory (`/home/jan/my_data/`).

The command uses the ssh protocol to encrypt the data. If not installed, install ssh with:

```
sudo apt-get install ssh
```

With a network connection to the Internet, the system can use a browser or other applications to access the Internet.

Communicating over Bluetooth

Bluetooth is an RF interface that supports wireless communications over distances of up to 10m (for Class 2 devices). A USB/Bluetooth bridge can provide access to devices and other computers with Bluetooth interfaces.

Like USB, Bluetooth supports communications for a variety of purposes. Each Bluetooth function has a profile that defines protocols for a specific function much as a USB class does. Defined profiles include serial port, file transfer, headset, and LAN access.

Bluetooth bridges, or dongles, can use the USB wireless controller class, subclass RF controller (01h), protocol Bluetooth Programming Interface (01h). With multiple interfaces, a single device can support multiple profiles. The Linux BlueZ protocol stack supports a variety of Bluetooth profiles.

The remote Bluetooth device can be a device with a specific function such as a headset, or the device may be a computer with a Bluetooth interface, which can be another USB/Bluetooth bridge.

Pairing to a Remote Device

Before communicating over Bluetooth, the two systems must discover each other and establish a pairing. Both systems must support the needed services for the desired function.

If not installed, install the bluez Bluetooth driver and related files with:

```
sudo apt-get install bluez python-gobject python-dbus
```

Every Bluetooth port has a 6-byte address that identifies the port to remote devices. The hcitool dev command displays the address of a local Bluetooth port. This example displays the address of an attached Bluetooth USB dongle:

```
hcitool dev
hci0    00:02:72:A5:E3:B2
```

hcitool scan returns the address and name of any remote devices detected.

This example displays the address of a Bluetooth USB dongle on a nearby PC named LVR1:

```
hcitool scan
00:02:72:A5:E3:6D  LVR1
```

The hciconfig tool displays information about local Bluetooth ports:

```
hciconfig
hci0: Type: BR/EDR  Bus: USB
  BD Address: 00:02:72:A5:E3:B2  ACL MTU: 1021:7  SCO MTU: 64:1
  UP RUNNING PSCAN ISCAN
  RX bytes:26824 acl:192 sco:0 events:239 errors:0
  TX bytes:9617 acl:194 sco:1 commands:54 errors:0
```

The ports are named beginning with hci0. Each port has an *inquiry scan* setting (ISCAN), which determines whether the port is visible to remote devices, and a *page scan* setting (PSCAN), which determines whether the port accepts requests to connect. This command enables both inquiry and page scans on hci0:

```
hciconfig hci0 piscan
```

The noscan option disables inquiry and page scans:

```
hciconfig hci0 noscan
```

The drivers for Bluetooth interfaces establish a pair by asking the systems to agree on a link key. Both ends of the link may display the link key and require the user to accept the key before establishing the pair.

Exchanging Data

The sdptool command displays the services available on a detected device with a specified address:

```
sdptool browse 00:02:72:A5:E3:6D
```

The command's output displays information obtained using the Bluetooth service discovery protocol. This portion of the command's output indicates device support for the OBEX File Transfer service.

```
Service Name: File Transfer
Service RecHandle: 0x10005
Service Class ID List:
  "OBEX File Transfer" (0x1106)
Protocol Descriptor List:
  "L2CAP" (0x0100)
  "RFCOMM" (0x0003)
    Channel: 4
  "OBEX" (0x0008)
```

```
Language Base Attr List:
  code_ISO639: 0x656e
  encoding:    0x6a
  base_offset: 0x100
Profile Descriptor List:
  "OBEX File Transfer" (0x1106)
    Version: 0x0100
```

The obexftp and obexpushd tools enable exchanging files with a remote computer using the OBEX protocol. If not installed, install the tools with:

sudo apt-get install obexftp obexpushd

This command sends the file test.txt to the Bluetooth port with the address specified:

obexftp -b 00:02:72:A5:E3:6D -p test.txt

This command listens to Bluetooth connections and enables receiving files from a remote port:

obexpushd -B

For GUI systems, an alternative to the command line is the gnome-bluetooth manager

If not installed, install with:

sudo apt-get install gnome-bluetooth

View the gnome-bluetooth manager from **System Settings > Internet and Network > Bluetooth**. To make the local system visible to Bluetooth devices, check the **Make computer visible** box. To enable communications with a new device, click **Set up new device** and follow the prompts. You can also access these functions by clicking the Bluetooth icon in the system tray.

To exchange files, click the Bluetooth icon in the top panel and select **Send Files to device or Browse Files on device**.

8

Printing

Embedded systems can use printers to print receipts, tickets, reports, and other documents. This chapter explains what's needed to support printing and provides an example Linux application.

Inside the Printer Class

USB hosts use bulk transfers to send data to printer-class devices. To retrieve status information, the host uses bulk transfers if the printer has a bulk IN endpoint or control transfers if not. In the printer's interface descriptor, bInterfaceClass = 07h.

Embedded Host Support

To print to a USB printer, the host system must support USB printer-class protocols. To enable printing more than plain text, the host should also support a printer control language that the target printer understands.

Some embedded-host platforms provide a function or class for sending raw data to a USB printer but leave it to the developer to add support for printer control languages or specific printer capabilities. Printer control languages have extensive capabilities and learning curves to match. A platform with full support for needed language(s) will simplify the task of programming printer communications. Linux has good support available for printing and printer control languages.

The limited resources of embedded systems mean that they can't support every feature of every printer, but an embedded system can support a defined set of printers and features.

Getting the Device ID

The USB printer-class request GET_DEVICE_ID can request a printer device ID that contains information about the printer and its capabilities. The IEEE 1284 interface standard defines the format of the device ID. The first two bytes are the ID's length in bytes, including the two length bytes, sent MSB first. Table 8-1 shows the three keys each device ID must contain.

Key Name (Full)	Key Name (Short)	Example
MANUFACTURER	MFR	MFG:Lakeview Research;
COMMAND SET	CMD	CMD:PJL,PCL,POSTCRIPT;
MODEL	MDL	MDL:USB Printer Model 100;

Table 8-1: Every device ID must contain these keys.

Each key contains the full or short version of the key name, which is case-sensitive, followed by one or more values in the format shown in the examples. Additional keys with information such as serial numbers are optional.

The example device ID below begins with two bytes that specify the ID's length of 70 bytes (46h) followed by 68 text characters containing the three required keys and their values:

```
0046
MFG:Lakeview Research;CMD:PJL,PCL,POSTCRIPT;MDL:USB Printer Model 100;
```

Host firmware can send the GET_DEVICE_ID request to a printer. The host typically requests two bytes to learn the length, followed by a request for the entire ID.

Alternatives

USB is the most common printer interface, but some printers have parallel, RS-232, or Ethernet ports in addition to or instead of USB ports. If your system has one of these interfaces and can use a compatible printer, you don't need a USB host. The system will still need to support any printer control languages the printer requires.

Printer Control Languages

Printer control languages define protocols for communicating with printers, including selecting fonts, printing images, using color, and more.

Popular printer control languages are ESC/P, Printer Command Language (PCL), PostScript, and languages that use Point of Service/Point of Sale (POS) protocols. The Printer Job Language (PJL) is a job-control language for managing printing at the job level.

Escape Sequences

Some printer languages send commands via escape sequences, where a special character or code indicates that the data that follows is a printer command. Many printers support basic escape sequences that begin with a backslash. For example, \f is the escape sequence that requests a form feed. Instead of printing "\f", the printer ejects the page. To print "\f", the host must send a double backslash: "\\f". Other common escape sequences are \n for line feed, \r for carriage return, and \t for tab.

The ESC/P language discussed below uses escape sequences that begin with the ASCII ESC code (1Bh).

Printing Plain Text

If you just need to print plain text, many printers will print received text characters followed by a form-feed code sent as the binary value 0Ch or as the text characters "\f". Line printers print a line of text after receiving a carriage-return code and eject the page on receiving a form-feed code.

ESC/P

Many printers support the ESC/P command language, which Epson Corporation developed for use with its dot-matrix line printers. ESC/P supports basic printer control and formatting. Most commands begin with an ESC code. The *Epson ESC/P Reference Manual* documents the commands.

Page Printer Languages

Most recent office printers, including laser and inkjet printers, are page printers that support PCL, PostScript, or both. Printers that support these languages may also support PJL. Receipt printers and other printers used in sales environments may use a language that supports POS protocols.

Some inexpensive printers are intended for use only with Windows hosts. The host uses the Windows Graphical Device Interface (GDI) and other software to convert each page's contents to bitmap data to send to the printer for printing. Even basic text transmits as bitmaps. These printers, require considerably more processing power on the host and thus are less suitable for embedded systems.

In the examples that follow, text in brackets (<>) refers to an ASCII code. For example, <LF> is a line-feed code (0Ah).

Printer Job Language

The Printer Job Language (PJL) defines job-level commands such as selecting a printer control language and receiving status information from the printer. Many recent PCL and PostScript printers also support PJL.

PJL commands begin with the @PJL prefix and end with a line feed (0Ah). A carriage return (0Dh) preceding the line feed is optional. HP recommends sending PJL commands only to printers that support PJL.

The Universal Exit Language (UEL) command restores user defaults and prints any partial page received. On printers that support PJL, the command prepares the printer to accept PJL commands. The command is:

`<ESC>%-12345X`

The JOB and EOJ commands bracket the start and end of a job.

`@PJL JOB<LF>`

`@PJL EOJ<LF>`

This command sets the printer language to PCL:

`@PJL ENTER LANGUAGE=PCL<LF>`

This command sets the printer language to PostScript:

`@PJL ENTER LANGUAGE=POSTSCRIPT<LF>`

For more about PJL, see HP's *Printer Job Language Technical Reference Manual*.

Printer Command Language

The Printer Command Language (PCL), developed by HP, defines commands that begin with an ESC code and end with the first upper-case letter that follows. PCL 5 defines commands for printer control and formatting and HP-GL/2 commands for printing vector graphics. Printers ignore unsupported commands.

PCL 6 added Enhanced PCL XL, a new language that uses binary encoding and is optimized for use with the Windows GDI. (A PCL 6 printer is not the same thing as a Windows-only printer as described below.) PCL 6 also incorporates PCL 5 commands under the name PCL 6 Standard. Compared to Enhanced PCL XL, PCL 5 has less overhead on the host and thus is more suitable for most embedded systems. The remainder of this discussion applies to PCL 5/PCL 6 Standard.

This example uses PCL and PJL to print the text, "This is a printer test." using the printer's default job and page settings:

```
<ESC>%-12345X<ESC>EThis is a printer test.<ESC>E<ESC>%-12345X
```

The Printer Reset command restores user defaults and prints any partial page received. The command is:

```
<ESC>E
```

In hex bytes, the sequence is:

```
1B 45
```

The UEL command does everything the Printer Reset command does, but HP recommends using both for backward compatibility. At the start of job, send the UEL command followed by the Printer Reset command. At the end of a job, send the Printer Reset command followed by the UEL command.

For more about PCL, see HP's *PCL 5 Printer Language Technical Reference Manual.*

PostScript

PostScript, developed by Adobe, is an interpreted programming language. A PostScript printer translates PostScript code to printer operations. Some printers support both PCL and PostScript.

This PostScript code prints the text, "This is a PostScript printer test.":

```
%!PS
/Courier 12 selectfont
72 720 moveto
(This is a PostScript printer test.) show
showpage
```

`%!` indicates the start of a comment. Beginning the file with a PostScript comment can help multi-language printers detect the language. Text following `%!` is optional.

The `selectfont` operator establishes the font and font size to use (12 pt Courier in the example).

The `moveto` operator specifies the current point, or where to start printing on the page. Measurements are in points. A point is 1/72 in. Location `0,0` is the lower left corner of the page. Assuming an 8.5 x 11 in. sheet, a current point setting of `72 720` starts printing 1 in. from the top and 1 in. from the left edge.

The text to print is in parentheses.

The `show` operator places the line of text on the page using the specified font, font size, and current point. The `showpage` operator tells the printer to print the page.

The Linux printing system is based on PostScript. For non-PostScript printers, Linux uses the Ghostscript program to convert PostScript code to a language the target printer understands.

For more about PostScript programming, see Adobe's *PostScript Language Reference*. Other references from Adobe are *The PostScript Language Tutorial and Cookbook* and *PostScript Language Program Design*.

Point-of-service Printer Languages

Many Point-of-Service (POS) printers support vendor-specific languages such as Epson's ESC/POS. The languages define commands for printer and job control and are suitable for embedded systems with limited resources. Because Epson is a major brand of POS printers, other printer brands often support ESC/POS. Systems running Windows Embedded for POS can use Microsoft's POS for .NET.

Debugging a Driver

When needed, a way to reverse-engineer a printer driver is to install the printer on a PC and in the printer dialog, select **Print to File**. When you print a document, the created file contains everything the PC would send to the printer. You can view the data in a hex editor. You'll likely find that the file contains a lot of overhead, much of it not essential for basic print jobs, but the file can provide a starting point of known working code for using a printer.

Printing Files

Linux systems can use the Common UNIX Printing System (CUPS), which supports commands and an API for printing formatted text and images. CUPS insulates you from having to know printer control languages. With CUPS, you can print many file types, including text, PDF, and image files. A CUPS backend supports printing to USB printers.

Using the Common Unix Printing System

References for using CUPS are *Introduction to CUPS Programming*, which includes documentation for the CUPS API, and *CUPS Software Users Manual*, which covers CUPS commands. Both documents are at *cups.org*.

To compile applications that use CUPS, the development system must have the cups library compiled for the target architecture.

On the target system, if not installed, install CUPS with:

`sudo apt-get install cups`

cups-doc includes a program with a web interface for administering printers:

`sudo apt-get install cups-doc`

After attaching a printer, restart the cups service if necessary with:

`sudo service cups stop`

`sudo service cups start`

With cups-doc installed, you can install and administer printers from a browser at:

`http://localhost:631/admin`

The browser program handles the details of finding attached printers and assigning appropriate drivers.

The /etc/cups/printers.conf file contains information about printers that have been installed, including printers that are no longer attached. Listing 8-1 shows an excerpt from a printers.conf file:

```
# Printer configuration file for CUPS v1.4.4
<DefaultPrinter Deskjet-460>
Info HP Deskjet 460
Location jan-desktop
MakeModel HP Deskjet 460, hpcups 3.10.6
DeviceURI hp:/usb/Deskjet_460?serial=MY648420BN
State Idle
StateTime 1291044569
Type 36876
Filter application/vnd.cups-raw 0 -
Filter application/vnd.cups-raster 0 hpcups
Accepting Yes
Shared Yes
JobSheets none none
QuotaPeriod 0
PageLimit 0
KLimit 0
OpPolicy default
ErrorPolicy retry-job
</Printer>
```

Listing 8-1: This excerpt from a printers.conf file shows the name (Deskjet-460) and other information about the system's default printer.

To see the status of all installed printers, at a command line, enter:

`lpstat -t`

The printer name(s) in the command's output match names in `printers.conf`:

`Deskjet-460 accepting requests since Fri 09 Sep 2011 01:00:03 PM CDT`

The `lpadmin` command can set the default printer:

`/usr/sbin/lpadmin -d Deskjet-460`

At the next print job, `printers.conf` will be updated to reflect the new default printer.

Additional tools for working with printers under Linux include:

Foomatic (*openprinting.org*), a database of printer drivers and a source of advice about installing printers.

The HP Linux Imaging and Printing (HPLIP) project (*hplipopensource.com*), which provides an installer and other tools for HP printers.

Sending a File to a Printer

Listing 8-2 uses the CUPS API to print a file.

```
#include <cups/cups.h>
#include <stdio.h>
#include <stdlib.h>
#include <string.h>

int main()
{
   char *file_to_print = "test.pdf";
   char *job_title = "Test Job";

   const char *cups_option_value;
   cups_dest_t *dest;
   cups_dest_t *dests;
   int job_id;
   int num_dests;

   num_dests = cupsGetDests(&dests);
   printf("num_dests = %d\n", num_dests);

   dest = cupsGetDest(NULL, NULL, num_dests, dests);
```

Listing 8-2: The CUPS API provides functions for printing. (Part 1 of 2)

```
    if (dest)
    {
        printf("Default printer: %s\n", dest->name);

        cups_option_value = cupsGetOption("printer-state",
          dest->num_options, dest->options);

        if (strtol(cups_option_value, NULL, 10) < IPP_PRINTER_STOPPED)
        {
            job_id = cupsPrintFile(
                    dest->name,
                    file_to_print,
                    job_title,
                    dest->num_options,
                    dest->options);
            printf("status = %s\n", cupsLastErrorString());
        }
        else
        {
            printf("Printer is stopped. Check printer.\n");
        }
    }
    else
    {
        printf ("No default printer.\n");
    }
    cupsFreeDests(num_dests, dests);
    return 0;
}
```

Listing 8-2: The CUPS API provides functions for printing. (Part 2 of 2)

Use the -lcups switch when compiling the application.

test.pdf is an existing file to print.

The CUPS function cupsGetDests accepts an address (&dests) for storing a list of structures that contain information about printers and other destinations such as a virtual printer that prints to PDF. The list may include printers that have been detected in the past but aren't currently attached. The function returns the number of destinations (num_dests).

The CUPS function cupsGetDest (note the singular "Dest") gets a specific destination in the list retrieved by cupsGetDests. The function accepts the name of the destination (NULL for the default printer), the destination's instance (NULL for the primary instance), the number of destinations to search (num_dests), and the list retrieved by cupsGetDests to search (dests).

Printer names are in /etc/cups/printers.conf in the Printer and DefaultPrinter fields. This example gets the destination "Deskjet-460":

```
dest = cupsGetDest("Deskjet-460", NULL, num_dests, dests);
```

Multiple instances of a printer can each have different default options. The lpoptions command can display printer options and define printer instances.

A destination retrieved with cupsGetDest isn't necessarily attached and available. To find out if the destination is available, cupsGetOption requests the printer-state value. When the printer is detached or otherwise unavailable, printer-state = IPP_PRINTER_STOPPED (05h). Other defined values are IPP_PRINTER_IDLE (03h) and IPP_PRINTER_PROCESSING (04h). The values are in the cups file ipp.h

The CUPS cupsPrintFile function prints a file to a destination. The function accepts the name field from the destination's structure (dest->name), the name of the file to print (file_to_print), a job name (job_title), and the num_options (dest->num_options) and options (dest->options) fields from the destination's structure. The function returns an ID number for the print job or zero on error.

After calling cupsPrintFile, cupsLastErrorString returns successful-ok or an error message.

The CUPS cupsFreeDests function frees the memory used by the list of destinations retrieved by cupsGetDests. The function accepts the number of destinations to free (num_dests) and a pointer to a list of destinations (dests). Call this function when finished using the printer.

9

Using Sound and Video

With support for the USB audio and video classes, embedded host systems can record and play audio and video with USB speakers, mics, and cameras. This chapter shows how.

Inside the Audio and Video Classes

Devices in the USB audio and video classes use isochronous transfers to carry real-time, streaming data. The audio class also supports using bulk transfers for MIDI data. Devices in both classes use class-specific descriptors to describe the device's capabilities in detail.

In an audio-class device's interface descriptor, bInterfaceClass = 01h. Devices in the USB audio class may comply with the USB audio class specification release 1.0 or 2.0. Release 1.0 supports high speed but with a maximum rate of one transaction/ms per transfer. Release 1.0 devices remain popular in part because Microsoft has delayed in providing a release 2.0 driver for Windows. USB audio 2.0 retains much of the framework defined in 1.0 but isn't backwards compatible. In other words, a release 2.0 device can't use a release 1.0 host driver. Release 2.0 requires using an interface association descriptor, adds new capabilities and controls, and provides full support for high speed, including transfers with multiple transactions/ms.

In a video-class device's interface descriptor, bInterfaceClass = 0Eh. Many webcams and other video devices belong to the USB video class.

Embedded Host Support

Built-in support for the audio and video classes is uncommon in embedded-host platforms. One reason might be the complexity of scheduling isochronous transfers on small systems. Streaming high-quality video requires a high-speed or SuperSpeed bus. Linux, including some distributions for embedded systems, supports USB audio and video. Chapter 10 shows how to use a display with a USB interface to show video (and other system screens).

Alternatives

On the BeagleBoard-xM, another option for audio input and output is the audio subsystem provided by the on-board Texas Instruments TPS65950 Integrated Power Management/Audio Codec. The BeagleBoard-xM also includes a dedicated camera port that connects to the processor's high-performance camera interface.

If you just need to transfer audio or video files, the mass storage class is an option that doesn't require isochronous transfers.

Playing and Recording Sound

Recent Linux kernels include the Advanced Linux Sound Architecture (ALSA) component that provides sound drivers and other support for audio functions. The ALSA applications aplay and arecord can play and record sounds. Other applications such as mplayer and lame have additional capabilities and support additional file formats.

Sound Cards

One or more "sound cards" provide audio functions. In an embedded system, the sound card likely isn't on a separate card but instead resides on the main processor's board or in an attached USB device.

You can view registered sound cards in the /proc/asound/cards file. Listing 9-1's example shows two sound cards:

```
0 [omap3beagle  ]: twl4030 - omap3beagle
                   omap3beagle (twl4030)
1 [default      ]: USB-Audio - USB  AUDIO
                   USB  AUDIO   at usb-ehci-omap.0-2.2, full speed
```

Listing 9-1: The /proc/asound/cards file lists available audio hardware.

Each entry consists of a card number (0, 1) followed by the card's name (omap3beagle, default), and additional information. In Listing 9-1, card 0 is the BeagleBoard-xM's onboard audio subsystem. (The TWL4030 is software compatible with the BeagleBoard's TPS65950). Card 1 is attached USB speakers.

The /dev/snd directory contains device nodes that applications may access for playing or recording sound using the sound cards. The USB speakers listed above have two device nodes:

controlC1 is the control device for card 1.

pcmC1D0p is the audio device for card 1, device 0. A single card can have multiple devices.

To identify which device nodes belong to a device, examine the /dev/snd directory before and after attaching the device.

Playing Sounds

The aplay application can play sounds in AU, RAW, VOC, or WAV formats. If not installed, install aplay (and other utilities) with:

sudo apt-get install alsa-utils

This command plays the file bittern.wav on card 1's device 0:

aplay -D plughw:1,0 bittern.wav

-D plughw:1,0 specifies the output device as card 1's device 0.

plughw is a plug-in layer that converts a file's sample format, sample frequency, and number of channels as needed to a format supported by the sound card.

The amixer application in alsa-utils can set the volume and other features of the sound card. The -c switch selects a sound card. This command sets the volume of card 1 (-c 1) to 40%:

amixer -c 1 set PCM 40%

The mute and unmute switches turn the audio on and off:

amixer -c 1 set PCM mute

amixer -c 1 set PCM unmute

An alternative to amixer's command-line interface is the graphical mixer application alsamixer.

The mplayer application supports additional file formats including MP3. If not installed, install mplayer with:

sudo apt-get install mplayer

This command plays an MP3 file:

mplayer -ao alsa:device=hw=1.0 sora.mp3

`-ao alsa:device=hw=1.0` specifies the audio output device (`-ao`) as card 1's device 0. `sora.mp3` is the file to play.

The `-af` option can set the volume:

```
mplayer -ao alsa:device=hw=1.0 -af volume=10 sora.mp3
```

`-af volume=10` sets a gain of 10 dB. A gain of `-200` mutes the sound. A gain of `vol-norm` gives maximum gain without distortion.

Listing 9-2 is an application that uses the `system` command to play a file with `mplayer`.

```
#include <stdlib.h>

int main()
{
    system ("mplayer -ao alsa:device=hw=1.0 sora.mp3");
    return 0;
}
```

Listing 9-2: The system command can launch the mplayer application.

You can also set `mplayer`'s options in a configuration file. System-wide settings are in `mplayer`'s directory, typically `/etc/mplayer/mplayer.conf`. User options are in the hidden `.mplayer` directory under the user's home directory, for example, `/home/jan/.mplayer/config`.

Recording

The `arecord` application included in `alsa-utils` can record sounds in AU, RAW, VOC, or WAV format.

The `amixer` application can set the volume for a mic:

```
amixer -c 2 set Mic 100%
```

`-c 2` selects card 2.

`Mic 100%` sets the desired gain.

This command records audio input from a USB mic to the file `blackbird.wav`:

```
arecord -D plughw:2,0 -r 16000 -f S16_LE -c 2 -d 3 blackbird.wav
```

`-D plughw:2,0` specifies the input device as card 2's device 0. The card and device numbers for the mic are in the `/dev/snd` directory described above.

`-r 16000` specifies a sampling rate of 16,000 Hz. The default is `8000`. A too-high sampling rate can result in underrun errors and dropouts.

`-f S16_LE` specifies signed 16-bit, little endian format.

-c 2 specifies using two input channels. The default is one channel.

-d 3 specifies recording for 3 seconds. If you eliminate this option or set it to zero, recording continues until the process ends via Ctrl+C or another means.

The MP3 format is popular in part because its compression dramatically reduces file size. The lame application can convert a raw file to a compressed file that MP3 players can play. Because MP3 technology is patented, you may need a license to include a compiled version of lame in a product.

If not installed, install lame with:

```
sudo apt-get install lame
```

This example records a raw file and pipes it to lame, which encodes the data and stores the result in a file:

```
arecord -D plughw:2,0 -r 16000 -f S16_LE -c 2 -t raw -d 3 | lame -s 16
    -r - blackbird.mp3
```

arecord records the file using the same options as the previous example plus the -t raw option to specify raw output format.

The lame application uses these options:

-s 16 sets a sampling frequency of 16,000 Hz.

-r specifies an input in raw pcm format.

- (hyphen alone) specifies using standard input as the input source. In this example, the standard input to lame is the output from arecord.

blackbird.mp3 stores the recorded mp3 file. Use mplayer as described above to play the file.

Playing and Recording Video

With USB video-class support and a display, an embedded-host system can play video captured by a USB camera. Systems can also record video for later playing on the same system or for transferring to another system for playing.

The Linux USB video class (UVC) driver included in recent kernels supports USB cameras that comply with the USB video class.

Showing Live Video

mplayer can also function as a movie player. This command displays live video from a USB camera:

```
mplayer tv:// -tv driver=v4l2:device=/dev/video0
```

tv:// specifies TV input, which includes input from USB video cameras.

`-tv driver=v4l2:device=/dev/video0` specifies using the Video4Linux2 driver (v4l2) and the camera's device node (/dev/video0).

The live video appears on the system's display. You can specify the frame width and height and frames per second (-fps) to display:

```
mplayer tv:// -tv driver=v4l2:width=640:height=480:
    device=/dev/video0 -fps 90
```

Recording

`mencoder` is a movie encoder that can record video from a USB camera for later playback

If not installed, install `mencoder` with:

```
sudo apt-get install mencoder
```

This command records video from a USB camera:

```
mencoder tv:// -tv driver=v4l2:width=320:height=240:fps=30:
    device=/dev/video0 -nosound -ovc lavc -lavcopts
    vcodec=mjpeg -o my_movie.avi
```

The `tv://` input and -tv options for driver, width, height, and device are the same as those options for mplayer.

`fps=30` is a driver option that specifies frames per second to capture (30).

`-nosound` disables sound recording.

`-ovc lavc` specifics using the `libavcodec` output video codec library (`lavc`) to encode the video.

`-lavcopts vcodec=mjpeg` specifies using the motion jpeg (`mjpeg`) encoding option for the lavc library.

`-o my_movie.avi` specifies saving the movie as `my_movie.avi`.

Playing Recorded Video

`mplayer` can play recorded video on the system's display:

```
mplayer -vfm ffmpeg my_movie.avi
```

`-vfm ffmpeg` specifies using the ffmpeg video decoder.

`my_movie.avi` is the file to play.

10

Communicating with Vendor-defined Devices

Most of the USB devices discussed so far fit defined USB device classes. The device declares a class in its descriptors, and the host system uses a class driver to access the device.

But some devices have vendor-defined functions that don't fit a standard class. Other devices have functions that might fit a class, but the target OS doesn't support the class or the device has features or abilities that the class driver doesn't support. An example of a class that lacks OS support is the test-and-measurement class. Because Windows doesn't include a class driver, many devices with test-and-measurement functions use vendor-defined drivers.

Another option for devices that exchange vendor-defined data is to use a USB class that enables transferring data for any purpose.

This chapter explores options for communicating with devices that perform vendor-defined functions.

Driver Options

Devices that don't use a standard class driver declare a vendor-defined function in the device descriptor (bDeviceClass = FFh) or an interface descriptor (bInterfaceClass = FFh). The host uses the device descriptor's Vendor ID and Product ID to match a driver to the device.

To access a device whose descriptors declare a vendor-defined function, a host system can use a custom driver tailored to the device's needs or a generic driver that can access device endpoints.

Custom Driver

A custom driver can provide exactly the capabilities needed to support a device's function. The driver can provide an API for sending device-specific commands in control requests and for exchanging other device-specific data using bulk, interrupt, and isochronous transfers as appropriate. The down side of this approach is the need to develop and maintain the driver.

Generic Driver

A generic driver enables accessing devices that don't have a class or custom driver. The driver typically provides an API for reading and writing to endpoints. An example of a generic driver is the libusb library for Linux and Windows.

A host may also use a generic driver to access devices that belong to a standard class. For example, Linux applications can use the libusb driver to access HID-class devices that transfer vendor-specific data.

Standard Class

Some devices with vendor-specific functions use a standard class driver that can transfer generic data for use by host applications. Suitable classes include communications, mass storage, and HID. A device that functions as a communications-class USB virtual serial port or Ethernet bridge can transfer data for any purpose. Mass-storage devices can transfer any kind of data in files. HID-class devices can transfer vendor-defined data in reports.

For these devices, the host must have the needed class driver and must understand the protocol for the vendor-defined data and provide an application to use the data.

Embedded Host Support

Providers of device-specific and generic drivers typically support major OSes only. An embedded-host platform may support a raw mode that functions like a generic driver, enabling the host to read and write to endpoints on any device. For example, the .NET Micro Framework library from GHI Electronics includes a RawDevice class that provides this capability. A host application can send and receive the vendor-specific data and put it to use.

If you need to provide a driver or application for a vendor-specific device, good documentation will save you from having to reverse-engineer the protocols.

Using a Generic Driver

The example Linux application below shows how to use the libusb generic driver to access a device with a vendor-defined function.

The libusb Library

The libusb library (*libusb.org*) provides an API for accessing device endpoints. The examples in this chapter use the libusb 1.0 API.

The application below communicates with a device designed for use with Microsoft's WinUSB generic driver. The application uses control, bulk, and interrupt transfers. Example PIC microcontroller firmware to use with this host code is at *janaxelson.com*.

To use libusb 1.0 functions, the development system must have the libusb-1.0.so library compiled for the target architecture and the header file libusb.h. The Ångström toolchain provides these files.

Look for libusb-1.0.so in:

/usr/local/angstrom/arm/arm-angstrom-linux-gnueabi/usr/lib/libusb-1.0

Look for libusb.h in:

/usr/local/angstrom/arm/arm-angstrom-linux-gnueabi/usr/include/
        libusb-1.0

To compile an application that uses libusb functions, use the -lusb-1.0 option to specify the lusb-1.0.so library. If you're compiling from a command line, use the -I switch if needed to specify the path to libusb.h. For example:

-I/usr/local/angstrom/arm/
        arm-angstrom-linux-gnueabi/usr/include/libusb-1.0

If using an IDE such as Eclipse, add the path to the project's Include paths.

Applications that use the libusb library to access devices require administrative privileges by default. Run the application with sudo or create a udev rule as described in Chapter 3.

Listing 10-1 shows the application's include statements, function prototypes, and constants.

```
#include <errno.h>
#include <string.h>
#include <stdio.h>
#include <stdlib.h>
#include <libusb.h>


int exchange_data_via_bulk_transfers(libusb_device_handle *devh);
int exchange_data_via_control_transfers(libusb_device_handle *devh);
int exchange_data_via_interrupt_transfers(libusb_device_handle
      *devh);


static const int INTERFACE_NUMBER = 0;
static const int TIMEOUT_MS = 5000;
```

Listing 10-1: The libusb application uses these include statements, functions, and constants.

INTERFACE_NUMBER equals bInteraceNumber in the interface descriptor for the desired interface.

TIMEOUT_MS sets a timeout in milliseconds for quitting a transfer.

Listing 10-2 is the application's main function.

```
int main(void)
{
   static const int VENDOR_ID = 0x0925;
   static const int PRODUCT_ID = 0x1456;

   struct libusb_device_handle *devh = NULL;
   int device_ready = 0;
   int result;

   result = libusb_init(NULL);
```

Listing 10-2: This libusb application exchanges data using control, bulk, and interrupt transfers. (Part 1 of 3)

```
if (result >= 0)
{
   devh = libusb_open_device_with_vid_pid(NULL, VENDOR_ID,
     PRODUCT_ID);
   if (devh != NULL)
   {
      {
         result = libusb_claim_interface(devh, 0);
         if (result >= 0)
         {
            device_ready = 1;
         }
         else
         {
            fprintf(stderr, "libusb_claim_interface error %d\n",
                    result);
         }
      }
   }
   else
   {
      fprintf(stderr, "Unable to find the device.\n");
   }
}
else
{
   fprintf(stderr, "Unable to initialize libusb.\n");
}
if (device_ready)
{
   exchange_data_via_control_transfers(devh);
   exchange_data_via_interrupt_transfers(devh);
   exchange_data_via_bulk_transfers(devh);

   libusb_release_interface(devh, 0);
}
```

Listing 10-2: This libusb application exchanges data using control, bulk, and interrupt transfers. (Part 2 of 3)

```
   libusb_close(devh);
   libusb_exit(NULL);
   return 0;
}
```

Listing 10-2: This libusb application exchanges data using control, bulk, and interrupt transfers. (Part 3 of 3)

The application obtains a handle to open the device, claims the interface, calls routines to exchange data using control, bulk, and interrupt transfers, and closes communications.

The VENDOR_ID and PRODUCT_ID constants should match the idVendor and idProduct values in the device descriptor of the target device:

libusb_init initializes the libusb driver. The parameter passed is a context value. For processes with a single user or module calling libusb functions, the context can be NULL. The libusb error codes are negative numbers, so a libusb function's return value greater than or equal to zero indicates success.

libusb_open_device_with_vid_pid attempts to open a device with the specified Vendor ID and Product ID. The first parameter is the context. On success, the function returns a handle to the first matching device found.

A successful call to libusb_claim_interface enables the application to exchange data with the device. The parameters passed are the device handle (devh) and the number of the desired interface (0). On success, the application calls the functions presented below to exchange data.

When finished communicating with the device, libusb_release_interface releases the interface, libusb_close closes the handle, and libusb_exit destroys the session.

Using Bulk Transfers

Listing 10-3's function uses bulk transfers to write data to a device and receive data from a device.

```
int exchange_data_via_bulk_transfers(libusb_device_handle *devh)
{
   static const int BULK_IN_ENDPOINT = 0x81;
   static const int BULK_OUT_ENDPOINT = 0x01;
   static const int MAX_BULK_IN_TRANSFER_SIZE = 64;
   static const int MAX_BULK_OUT_TRANSFER_SIZE = 64;
```

Listing 10-3: This function exchanges generic data using bulk transfers. (Part 1 of 3)

```
int bytes_transferred;
char data_in[MAX_BULK_IN_TRANSFER_SIZE];
char data_out[MAX_BULK_OUT_TRANSFER_SIZE];
int i;
int result = 0;

strcpy(data_out, "Bulk transfer test data.");
result = libusb_bulk_transfer(
    devh,
    BULK_OUT_ENDPOINT,
    data_out,
    strlen(data_out),
    &bytes_transferred,
    TIMEOUT_MS);

if (result >= 0)
{
   printf("Data sent via bulk transfer:\n");
   for(i = 0; i < bytes_transferred; i++)
   {
      printf("%c",data_out[i]);
   }
   printf("\n");

   result = libusb_bulk_transfer(
       devh,
       BULK_IN_ENDPOINT,
       data_in,
       MAX_BULK_IN_TRANSFER_SIZE,
       &bytes_transferred,
       TIMEOUT_MS);
```

Listing 10-3: This function exchanges generic data using bulk transfers. (Part 2 of 3)

```
     if (result >= 0)
   {
      if (bytes_transferred > 0)
      {
         printf("Data received via bulk transfer:\n");
         for(i = 0; i < bytes_transferred; i++)
         {
            printf("%c",data_in[i]);
         }
         printf("\n");
      }
      else
      {
         fprintf(stderr, "No data received in bulk transfer (%d)\n",
                 result);
         return -1;
      }
   }
   else
   {
      fprintf(stderr, "Error receiving data via bulk transfer
              %d\n", result);
      return result;
   }
}
else
{
   fprintf(stderr, "Error sending data via bulk transfer %d\n",
           result);
   return result;
}
return 0;
}
```

Listing 10-3: This function exchanges generic data using bulk transfers. (Part 3 of 3)

The function accepts a pointer to a `libusb` device handle and returns zero on success or a libusb error code on failure. The function communicates with a device with known endpoint addresses (81h and 01h) and maximum transfer sizes (64 bytes).

The libusb function `libusb_bulk_transfer` sends and requests data using bulk transfers. To send data to the device, the function passes these parameters:

A handle to the device (`devh`).

The endpoint's address (`BULK_OUT_ENDPOINT`).

A buffer to hold the data to send (`data_out`)

The number of bytes to write (`strlen(data_out)`).

The address of a variable that will store the number of bytes transferred (`&bytes_transferred`).

A timeout value in milliseconds (`TIMEOUT_MS`).

To request data from the device, the function passes these parameters:

A handle to the device (`devh`).

The endpoint address (`BULK_IN_ENDPOINT`).

A buffer to hold the received data (`data_in`).

The maximum number of bytes to read (`MAX_BULK_IN_TRANSFER_SIZE`).

The address of a variable that will hold the number of bytes transferred (`&bytes_transferred`).

A timeout value in milliseconds (`TIMEOUT_MS`).

Using Interrupt Transfers

In a similar way, Listing 10-4's function uses interrupt transfers to write data to a device and receive data from the device.

```
int exchange_data_via_interrupt_transfers(libusb_device_handle *devh)
{
    static const int INTERRUPT_IN_ENDPOINT = 0x82;
    static const int INTERRUPT_OUT_ENDPOINT = 0x02;
    static const int MAX_INTERRUPT_IN_TRANSFER_SIZE = 2;
    static const int MAX_INTERRUPT_OUT_TRANSFER_SIZE = 2;
```

Listing 10-4: This function exchanges generic data using interrupt transfers (Part 1 of 3)

```
int bytes_transferred;
char data_in[MAX_INTERRUPT_IN_TRANSFER_SIZE];
char data_out[MAX_INTERRUPT_OUT_TRANSFER_SIZE];
int i = 0;
int result = 0;

for (i=0;i < MAX_INTERRUPT_OUT_TRANSFER_SIZE; i++)
{
    data_out[i]=0x40+i;
}

result = libusb_interrupt_transfer(
        devh,
        INTERRUPT_OUT_ENDPOINT,
        data_out,
        MAX_INTERRUPT_OUT_TRANSFER_SIZE,
        &bytes_transferred,
        TIMEOUT_MS);

if (result >= 0)
{
    printf("Data sent via interrupt transfer:\n");
    for(i = 0; i < bytes_transferred; i++)
    {
        printf("%02x ",data_out[i]);
    }
    printf("\n");

    result = libusb_interrupt_transfer(
            devh,
            INTERRUPT_IN_ENDPOINT,
            data_in,
            MAX_INTERRUPT_OUT_TRANSFER_SIZE,
            &bytes_transferred,
            TIMEOUT_MS);
```

Listing 10-4: This function exchanges generic data using interrupt transfers (Part 2 of 3)

```
        if (result >= 0)
        {
            if (bytes_transferred > 0)
            {
                printf("Data received via interrupt transfer:\n");
                for(i = 0; i < bytes_transferred; i++)
                {
                    printf("%02x ",data_in[i]);
                }
                printf("\n");
            }
            else
            {
                fprintf(stderr, "No data received in interrupt transfer
                        (%d)\n", result);
                return -1;
            }
        }
        else
        {
            fprintf(stderr, "Error receiving data via interrupt transfer
                    %d\n", result);
            return result;
        }
    }

    else
    {
        fprintf(stderr, "Error sending data via interrupt transfer
                %d\n", result);
        return result;
    }
    return 0;
}
```

Listing 10-4: This function exchanges generic data using interrupt transfers (Part 3 of 3)

Chapter 10

The function accepts a pointer to a `libusb` device handle and returns zero on success or a `libusb` error code on failure.

From the application's perspective, interrupt transfers are identical to bulk transfers. The differences are in scheduling by the host controller and allowed maximum packet sizes. Thus the function above is much like the function for doing bulk transfers. The endpoint addresses and maximum transfer sizes are set to match the desired endpoints (82h and 02h) and transfer sizes (2 bytes).

The libusb function `libusb_interrupt_transfer` sends or receives data using interrupt transfers. The example transfers binary data instead of the string used in the previous example, but either transfer type can send and receive any type of data.

Using Control Transfers

Listing 10-5's function uses control transfers to exchange data with a device.

```
int exchange_data_via_control_transfers(libusb_device_handle *devh)
{
    static const int CONTROL_REQUEST_TYPE_IN = LIBUSB_ENDPOINT_IN |
            LIBUSB_REQUEST_TYPE_VENDOR | LIBUSB_RECIPIENT_INTERFACE;
    static const int CONTROL_REQUEST_TYPE_OUT = LIBUSB_ENDPOINT_OUT |
            LIBUSB_REQUEST_TYPE_VENDOR | LIBUSB_RECIPIENT_INTERFACE;

    static const int MAX_CONTROL_IN_TRANSFER_SIZE = 8;
    static const int MAX_CONTROL_OUT_TRANSFER_SIZE = 8;

    static const int WINUSB_REQUEST_1 = 0x01;
    static const int WINUSB_REQUEST_2 = 0x02;

    int bytes_received;
    int bytes_sent;
    char data_in[MAX_CONTROL_IN_TRANSFER_SIZE];
    char data_out[MAX_CONTROL_OUT_TRANSFER_SIZE];int i = 0;
    int result = 0;
```

Listing 10-5: This function uses control transfers to exchange generic data with a device. (Part 1 of 3)

```
for (i=0;i < MAX_CONTROL_OUT_TRANSFER_SIZE; i++)
{
    data_out[i]=0x30+i;
}
bytes_sent = libusb_control_transfer(
        devh,
        CONTROL_REQUEST_TYPE_OUT,
        WINUSB_REQUEST_1,
        0,
        INTERFACE_NUMBER,
        data_out,
        sizeof(data_out),
        TIMEOUT_MS);

if (bytes_sent >= 0)
{
    printf("Data sent via control transfer:\n");
    for(i = 0; i < bytes_sent; i++)
    {
        printf("%02x ",data_out[i]);
    }
    printf("\n");
    bytes_received = libusb_control_transfer(
        devh,
        CONTROL_REQUEST_TYPE_IN,
        WINUSB_REQUEST_2,
        0,
        INTERFACE_NUMBER,
        data_in,
        MAX_CONTROL_IN_TRANSFER_SIZE,
        TIMEOUT_MS);
```

Listing 10-5: This function uses control transfers to exchange generic data with a device. (Part 2 of 3)

```
    if (bytes_received >= 0)
    {
        printf("Data received via control transfer:\n");
        for(i = 0; i < bytes_received; i++)
        {
            printf("%02x ",data_in[i]);
        }
        printf("\n");
    }
    else
    {
        fprintf(stderr, "Error receiving data via control transfer
            %d\n", result);
        return result;
    }
}

else
{
    fprintf(stderr, "Error sending data via control transfer %d\n",
        result);
    return result;
}
return 0;
}
```

Listing 10-5: This function uses control transfers to exchange generic data with a device. (Part 3 of 3)

The function accepts a pointer to a libusb device handle and returns zero on success or a libusb error code on failure.

The function communicates with a device with known maximum transfer sizes for the vendor-specific control requests (8 bytes) and two supported control requests (01h and 02h).

The libusb function libusb_control_transfer initiates a control transfer. For a control transfer that sends data to the device in the Data stage, the function passes these parameters:

A handle to the device (devh).

bmRequestType in the Setup packet (CONTROL_REQUEST_TYPE_OUT).

bRequest in the Setup packet (`WINUSB_REQUEST_1`).

wValue in the Setup packet (`0`).

wIndex in the Setup packet (`INTERFACE_NUMBER`).

A buffer to hold the data to send (`data_out`).

The number of bytes to write (`sizeof(data_out)`).

A timeout value in milliseconds (`TIMEOUT_MS`).

For a control transfer that requests data from the device in the Data stage, the function passes these parameters:

A handle to the device (`devh`).

bmRequestType in the Setup packet (`CONTROL_REQUEST_TYPE_IN`).

bRequest in the Setup packet (`WINUSB_REQUEST_2`).

wValue in the Setup packet (`0`).

wIndex in the Setup packet (`INTERFACE_NUMBER`).

A buffer to hold received data (`data_in`).

The maximum number of bytes to read (`MAX_CONTROL_IN_TRANSFER_SIZE`).

A timeout value in milliseconds (`TIMEOUT_MS`).

See Chapter 1 for details on the fields in the Setup packet.

Accessing Vendor-defined HID-class Devices

Some HID-class devices are "generic" devices that don't function as keyboards, mice, or other system devices but instead send and receive vendor-specific data. In Linux, applications have several options for exchanging data with these devices.

The hidapi library (*signal11.us/oss/hidapi*) provides a HID-specific API for communicating with HIDs. The library has two implementations: a libusb implementation based on libusb 1.0 and a hidraw implementation based on the Linux hidraw driver.

A third option is to use the `libusb_release_interface` function to detach the HID driver from a device and use libusb functions to access the device's endpoints much as the example above does. However, the developers of libusb 1.0 recommend using hidapi functions to access HIDs.

The example below uses the libusb implementation of hidapi.

Development System Requirements

For cross-compiling a hidapi/libusb application, the development PC must have the hidapi library files and support for `libusb 1.0` as described for the application above.

To obtain the hidapi files, follow the instructions at *signal11.us/oss/hidapi* and store the files in your chosen location on the development PC.

The hidapi files include an example `hidtest` application that displays information about all installed HIDs, opens a handle to a HID with a specific Vendor ID and Product ID, and sends and receives Input, Output, and Feature reports.

The Device

The provided hidapi application communicates with a device running the generic HID firmware included in Microchip's Application libraries. An alternate version of the application and generic HID PIC firmware are available at *janaxelson.com*.

Cross-compiling the Application

Here is one way to cross-compile `hidtest`:

1. Copy `hidtest.cpp` and `hid-libusb.c` into your project's directory.

`hidtest.cpp` is in:

your_installation_directory/hidapi/hidtest/

where *your_installation_directory*/hidapi is the directory containing the hidapi files.

`hid-libusb.c` is in:

your_installation_directory/hidapi/linux/

2. Copy `hidapi.h` into your project's include directory (or the project's main directory).

`hidapi.h` is in:

your_installation_directory/hidapi/hidapi/

3. Include the path to `libusb.h`. Look for `libusb.h` in:

/usr/local/angstrom/arm/arm-angstrom-linux-gnueabi/usr/include/
      libusb-1.0

4. Compile `hidtest.cpp` and `hid-libusb.c` using the `-lusb-1.0` option.

At a command line, use:

your_gcc_cross_compiler **-I** *path_to_libusb.h* **hidtest.cpp hid-libusb.c**
      -lusb-1.0 -o hidtest

where *your_gcc_cross_compiler* invokes the cross-compiler for your target system and *path_to_libusb.h* is the directory containing `libusb.h`.

For example:

```
arm-angstrom-linux-gnueabi-gcc -I/usr/local/angstrom/arm/arm-ang-
    strom-linux-gnueabi/usr/include/libusb-1.0 hidtest.cpp
    hid-libusb.c -lusb-1.0 -o hidtest
```

As always, you can automate the process using a `makefile` or an IDE such as Eclipse.

Running the Application

To test the application, copy the created `hidtest` binary file to the target USB host system and attach a device running the generic HID firmware described above.

Run the application with `sudo` or create a `udev` rule as described in Chapter 3.

Follow the same procedure to compile other hidapi applications you write, replacing `hidtest.cpp` with your own source file.

Using a USB Display Monitor

For systems that need a display monitor, a display with a USB interface eliminates the need to have a DVI-D port or other display interface. USB displays don't fit a standard USB class and thus use vendor-specific drivers.

The Display

Lilliput Electronics Co., Ltd offers a 7-in. display with a high-speed USB interface (Figure 10-1). The display uses a DisplayLink USB graphics processor and a vendor-specific USB host driver. A Linux driver for the DisplayLink processor is available.

The display draws its power entirely from the bus. The attached cable has two USB connectors but enumerates as a single device with the second connector apparently used only for additional power. The device must attach to host or hub ports that can provide the 500 mA the device requests in its configuration descriptor.

Installing the Driver

The DisplayLink wiki at *libdlo.freedesktop.org/wiki* has links to detailed instructions for compiling and installing the display's driver and related software. In addition to the driver, the device requires a configuration file titled `xorg.conf` stored in `/etc/X11/`.

Figure 10-1. This 7-in. display monitor connects via USB.

Listing 10-6 shows an example configuration file.

```
# xorg.conf (X.Org X Window System server configuration file)

Section "ServerLayout"
    Identifier     "Server Layout"
    Screen 0       "DisplayLinkScreen" 0 0
    Option         "Xinerama" "Off"
EndSection

Section "Files"
    ModulePath     "/usr/lib/xorg/modules"
    ModulePath     "/usr/local/lib/xorg/modules"
    ModulePath     "/usr/local/lib/xorg/modules/drivers"
EndSection
```

Listing 10-6: This xorg.conf file contains configuration settings for a USB display. (Part 1 of 2)

```
Section "Device"
    Identifier      "DisplayLinkDevice"
    driver          "displaylink"
    Option          "fbdev" "/dev/fb3"
EndSection

Section "Monitor"
    Identifier      "DisplayLinkMonitor"
EndSection

Section "Screen"
    Identifier      "DisplayLinkScreen"
    Device          "DisplayLinkDevice"
    Monitor         "DisplayLinkMonitor"
    DefaultDepth    16
    SubSection      "Display"
        Depth       16
        Modes       "800x480"
    EndSubSection
EndSection
```

Listing 10-6: This xorg.conf file contains configuration settings for a USB display. (Part 2 of 2)

In the file's ServerLayout section, the Screen item designates Screen 0 as an active screen with the Identifier "DisplayLinkScreen" and absolute x and y coordinates of 0, 0 (the upper left corner). An Option item turns off the Xinerama extension, which isn't compatible with the DisplayLink driver.

The Files section provides paths to driver files.

The Device section has the Identifier "DisplayLinkDevice" and names the device's driver (displaylink). An Option item specifies using the Xorg driver for framebuffer devices (fbdev) for the screen's device node (/dev/fb3).

On the BeagleBoard-xM, you can use a display connected to the DVI-D port to find the USB screen's device node. With the device detached, enter:

```
ls /dev/fb*
```

You should see something like this:

```
/dev/fb0  /dev/fb1  /dev/fb2
```

Attach the device and repeat the command. The new file (/dev/fb3 below) is the screen's device node:

/dev/fb0 /dev/fb1 /dev/fb2 /dev/fb3

The Monitor section has the Identifier "DisplayLinkMonitor" and no additional items.

The Screen section ties the sections together. The DisplayLinkScreen identifier matches the setting for Screen 0 in the ServerLayout section. The Device and Monitor items identify the Device and Monitor sections to use for Screen 0. The section also specifies a color depth and resolution for the screen.

A system with the appropriate configuration file and drivers loaded will use the display as the system monitor.

11

Implementing a Dual-role Port

Chapter 2 introduced USB On-The-Go (OTG), which uses a single port to perform both host and device functions. This chapter explains OTG requirements and protocols and shows how to use an OTG port as a host and device port.

Inside USB On-The-Go (OTG)

The USB-IF's *On-The-Go and Embedded Host Supplement to the USB Revision 2.0 Specification* defines a way for a system to function as both a limited-capability host and a peripheral, switching roles as needed. When connected to a USB host, the OTG port functions as a device port. When connected to a peripheral on the system's Targeted Peripheral List, the OTG port functions as a host port. For example, a camera might function as a device that connects to a host for uploading images and a host that connects to a printer for printing photos.

Compared to host-only ports, OTG adds complexity by requiring the ability to function as a peripheral and requiring support for protocols that enable swapping roles. OTG reduces hardware cost and size by using a single connector for both functions.

Requirements

To support OTG, the system must have an OTG hardware port and support for protocols for role switching. Table 11-1 compares the requirements of a conventional host and an OTG system functioning as a host.

Capability or Feature	USB 2.0 Conventional Host	USB 2.0 OTG system Functioning as a Host
Communicate at high speed	Yes	As needed to support targeted peripherals
Communicate at full speed	Yes	Yes
Communicate at low speed	Yes	As needed to support targeted peripherals (not allowed when operating as a peripheral)
Support external hubs	Yes	Optional
Provide Targeted Peripheral List	No	Yes
Function as a peripheral	Requires a separate device port	Yes, when not functioning as a host
Support Attach Detection Protocol (ADP)	Optional	Optional
Support Session Request Protocol (SRP)	Optional	Yes if the device supports HNP as a B-device; otherwise optional
Support Host Negotiation Protocol (HNP)	No	Yes as an A-device; yes as a B-device if the Targeted Peripheral List includes an OTG system
Minimum available bus current per port	500 mA (100 mA if battery-powered)	8 mA or the amount needed by targeted peripherals, whichever is greater
OK to turn off VBUS when unneeded?	No	Yes
Connectors	1 or more Standard-A	1 Micro-AB

Table 11-1: USB 2.0 OTG hosts have different requirements compared to conventional USB hosts.

An OTG host doesn't have to support external hubs, multiple devices attached at the same time, or low and high speeds.

When functioning as a host, the OTG system can communicate with the devices in its Targeted Peripheral List (defined in Chapter 2). The targeted peripherals can be any combination of other OTG systems and peripheral-only devices.

OTG communications occur in sessions. A session begins when VBUS rises above the session-valid threshold voltage and ends when VBUS falls below this voltage. To conserve power, an OTG system that is providing power on VBUS can remove bus power when the bus is idle.

The OTG Connector

An OTG system has one and only one Micro-AB receptacle, which can accept a Micro-A plug or a Micro-B plug. The USB-IF has deprecated the larger Mini-AB receptacle defined in the OTG 1.0 specification, but the connector remains in use. The BeagleBoard-xM uses the Mini-AB receptacle (Figure 11-1).

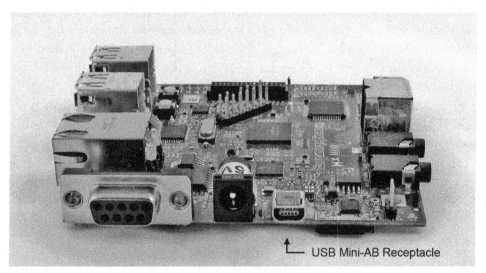

USB Mini-AB Receptacle

Figure 11-1. The BeagleBoard-xM has a Mini-AB connector for its OTG port.

Any references to the Micro-series connectors in this book also apply to the Mini series. For SuperSpeed OTG systems, the USB 3.0 specification defines a USB 3.0 Micro-AB receptacle and USB 3.0 Micro-A plug.

The Micro-A and Micro-B plugs include an ID pin that enables an OTG system to detect whether an Micro-A or Micro-B plug is inserted. On the Micro-B plug, the ID pin is open or connected to the ground pin by a resistance greater than 100kΩ On the Micro-A plug, the ID pin connects to the GND pin (Figure 11-2).

Figure 11-2. On the Micro-A plug, the ID pin connects to ground. On the Micro-B plug, the ID pin has a resistance > 100KΩ to ground.

The A-Device and B-Device

Every connection to an OTG port is between an A-device and a B-device. An OTG port with a Micro-A plug inserted is an A-Device. The system at the other end of the cable, which can be another OTG system or a conventional peripheral, is the B-device. On attachment, the A-device functions as the host, and the B-device functions as the peripheral. Two connected OTG systems can use the Host Negotiation Protocol to swap roles. The A-device is always the source of VBUS even when functioning as a peripheral. An OTG system must detect the resistance at the OTG connector's ID pin and implement the host or device function accordingly.

To connect an OTG system to a conventional host, use a cable with a Micro-B plug for the OTG port and a Standard-A plug for the host. When connected to a conventional host, the OTG system functions as a peripheral.

To connect an OTG port to a conventional peripheral, use a cable with a Micro-A plug for the OTG and a mating B-series plug for the device. Or you can use an adapter with a Micro-A plug and a Standard-A receptacle (Figure 11-3) along with a cable that has a Standard-A plug and a series-B plug.

Figure 11-3. This adapter enables connecting an OTG system with a Mini-AB receptacle to a conventional USB host using a cable with a Standard-A plug.

The *On-The-Go and Embedded Host Supplement* approves the use of this adapter. When connected to a conventional peripheral, the OTG system functions as a host only.

Responsibilities

A USB 2.0 OTG system must provide all of the following:

- The ability to function as a full-speed peripheral. Support for high speed is optional. The peripheral function must not use low speed.
- The ability to function as a host that can communicate with one or more full-speed devices. Support for low and high speeds and hubs is optional.
- A Targeted Peripheral List. (See Chapter 2.)
- When functioning as an A-device, support for the Host Negotiation Protocol (HNP) for role swapping. When functioning as a B-device, support for HNP if the Targeted Peripheral List includes any OTG systems.
- If the device ever turns off Vbus with a Micro-A plug inserted, the ability to respond to the Session Request Protocol (SRP). If the device supports HNP when functioning as a B-device, the ability to initiate SRP.
- Support for remote wakeup.
- One and only one Micro-AB receptacle.
- When functioning as the A-device, the ability to provide the bus current required by the targeted peripherals.
- A display, indicators, or other way to communicate with users.

The OTG Descriptor

The OTG descriptor enables the host to learn whether an attached B-device supports the Attach Detection Protocol (ADP), Host Negotiation Protocol (HNP), and Session Request Protocol (SRP). Any B-device that supports ADP, HNP, or SRP must return an OTG descriptor in response to a Get Descriptor request for the configuration descriptor.

The OTG specification doesn't say where to insert the descriptor, but typically the OTG system returns the OTG descriptor immediately following the configuration descriptor. The system must also return the descriptor in response to a Get_Descriptor(OTG) request.

Table 11-2 shows the contents of the descriptor.

Offset	Field	Size	Description
0	bLength	1	Descriptor length (05h)
1	bDescriptorType	1	OTG (09h)

2	bmAttributes	1	Protocols supported as B-device:
			D0 1 = SRP supported,
			       0 = SRP not supported
			D1 1 = HNP supported,
			       0 = HNP not supported
			D2 1 = ADP supported,
			       0 = ADP not supported
			D3–D7 reserved

3	bcdOTG	2	OTG and EH supplement revision number in BCD format (release 2.0 = 0200h). This field is present only if the revision number >= 2.

Table 11-2: The OTG descriptor informs the host about support for OTG protocols.

The bmAttributes field tells whether the device supports HNP, SRP, and ADP. The A-device doesn't need to know in advance if a device supports SRP, but the descriptor provides the information for use in compliance testing.

For more about ADP and SRP, see Chapter 2.

Host Negotiation Protocol (HNP)

An OTG system functioning as a peripheral can use the Host Negotiation Protocol (HNP) to request to function as the host.

When two OTG systems connect to each other, the A-device enumerates the B-device in the same way that a standard USB host enumerates its devices. During enumeration, the A-device retrieves the B-device's OTG descriptor, which indicates whether the B-device supports HNP.

If the B-device supports HNP, the A-device can send a Set_Feature control request with a request code of b_hnp_enable (03h). The request informs the B-device that it can use HNP to request to function as the host when the bus is suspended.

At any time after enumerating, an A-device that has no communications for the B-device can suspend the bus. The B-device can then use HNP to request to communicate. The B-device might use HNP in response to user input such as pressing a button, or firmware can initiate HNP without user intervention.

Support for HNP ensures that an OTG B-device can request to communicate with the peripheral function of an attached and supported OTG system. If the Targeted Peripheral List includes no OTG systems, the OTG B-device isn't required to support HNP because the supported peripherals will never use it.

Standard hubs don't recognize HNP signaling. If a hub is between the A-device and the B-device, the A-device must not send the hnp_enable request and the B-device can't use HNP.

When idle or functioning as a host, an OTG system should switch in its pull-down resistors on D+ and D-. When functioning as a peripheral, an OTG system should disable its pull-down resistor on D+ only.

Requesting to Operate as a Host

This is the protocol the B-device uses to request to operate as the host:

1. The A-device suspends the bus.

2. If the devices were communicating at full speed, the B-device removes itself from the bus by switching out its pull-up resistor on D+. If the devices were communicating at high speed, the B-device enters full-speed mode by switching in its pull-up on D+ briefly, then switches the pull-up out. The bus segment is then in the single-ended zero (SE0) state.

3. The A-device detects the SE0 state and connects to the bus as a device by switching in its pull-up resistor on D+, placing the bus segment in the J state.

4. The B-device detects the J state and resets the bus.

5. The B-device enumerates the A-device and can perform other communications with the device.

Returning to Operation as a Peripheral

When finished communicating, the B-device returns to its role as a peripheral using the following protocol:

1. The B-device stops all bus activity and may switch in its pull-up resistor.

2. The A-device detects a lack of activity for at least 3 ms, enters full-speed mode if communicating at high speed, and switches out its pull-up resistor or removes VBUS to end the session.

3. If VBUS is present and the B-device didn't switch in its pull-up in Step 1, the B-device switches in its pull-up to connect as a peripheral.

4. If VBUS is present, the A-device can reset the bus and enumerate and communicate with the B-device or end the session by removing VBUS.

Requesting Device Status

During an active OTG session, a host determines if a device wants to function as a host by initiating a control transfer with a Get_Status request with wIndex = F000h. In the Data stage of the request, the device returns 01h if the device wants to function as the host or 00h if not. During active sessions between two OTG systems, the host must issue the request every 1–2 s. On receiving a request to function as the host, the currently active host must suspend the bus within 2 s to enable the remote device to initiate HNP.

Supporting OTG Functions

Many processors and USB interface chips with Embedded Host ports also support OTG functions. Sources for microcontrollers and other processors with on-chip OTG support include Cypress Semiconductor, Freescale Semiconductor Inc., Microchip Technology, and Texas Instruments. Sources for external host interface chips with OTG ports include PLX Technology and ST-Ericsson.

Linux Drivers

PCs generally don't have OTG ports (or device ports), but Linux distributions for embedded systems may include drivers for OTG controllers. The driver for the BeagleBoard-xM's OTG port is the musb_hdrc module, which integrates hardware based on the Mentor Graphics high-speed OTG USB core with Linux kernels 2.6.x.

To enable using the OTG port as a host port, the system must load the musb_hdrc driver. To enable using the OTG port as a device port, the system must load a USB gadget driver for the desired device function as described below.

Power Management

A power-management chip can support enabling VBUS on detecting an attached A-device and waking the system on detecting the presence of VBUS.

An example is the Texas Instruments TPS65950 power management and system companion device. The chip controls VBUS according to the detected resistance on the ID pin and detects a change from VBUS removed to VBUS present. The chip also supports using the OTG port to provide power for accessories as defined in the CEA-936-A USB Carkit protocols, which enable using the USB port for hands-free operation of mobile phones.

Implementing a Peripheral Function

The Linux USB gadget API enables a system with a USB OTG port (or USB device port) to function as a USB device.

Support

The most basic Linux USB gadget is gadget zero, which supports one bulk IN endpoint and one bulk OUT endpoint. Other supported devices include a variety of Ethernet adapters, virtual serial port, MIDI device, mass storage, and gadgetFS for vendor-defined devices.

Linux support for OTG functions and protocols may be incomplete even in distributions intended for systems with OTG ports. If you want to use OTG functions, be sure your system can provide the capabilities you need. On the BeagleBoard-xM, the Ångström distribution has had better support for OTG functions and protocols compared to the Ubuntu Netbook distribution.

On the BeagleBoard-xM, which has four host ports and supports external hubs, the main use for the OTG port is to enable the board to function as a USB device. But the OTG port provides a way to test OTG functions for products that will contain only an OTG port.

A Mass-storage Device

An OTG system that emulates a drive provides a way to share data with host systems. For example, an OTG system can store data in files, and on attachment to a USB host, the host can access the files on the emulated drive. Or a host can store data on an OTG system's emulated drive, and the OTG system can use the data after detaching from the host.

To implement a mass-storage device using the gadget driver, you need to specify where the emulated drive will store data. One option is to designate and configure a special file called a backing file. The file's size equals the desired size of the storage media. A drive partition can also serve as a backing file.

Using a file as a backing file for a USB mass-storage device requires these steps:

1. Create the file.

2. Format the file to emulate a drive.

3. Create a file system on the emulated drive.

4. Assign the file as the backing file for the emulated drive.

5. Attach the emulated drive to a USB host system.

137

The host system can then access the file as if it were a drive, creating, accessing, moving, and deleting files and directories.

Do steps 1, 2, and 3 once to create the emulated drive. The system containing the emulated drive must perform step 4 on every boot up before communicating with a USB host.

Here are details about each step.

1. Create the File

The dd command creates a file named gadget_drive that is a copy of the /dev/zero file for the gadget zero device but with a size of 4 MB (4 blocks of 1 MB each).

```
dd bs=1M count=4 if=/dev/zero of=gadget_drive
4+0 records in
4+0 records out
4194304 bytes (4.2 MB) copied, 0.144439 s, 29.0 MB/s
```

2. Format the File to Emulate a Drive

Even though a file has no actual cylinders, sectors, or heads, the host expects the file to be structured like a physical drive. To format the emulated drive, run fdisk on the created file, and at the prompt, enter x to enter expert mode.

fdisk is a powerful tool that can destroy all data on a drive. When you run fdisk, be sure you specify the file that will hold your emulated drive (gadget_drive) and not a crucial system drive!

The text in the responses to the fdisk commands below may vary with the version of fdisk.

```
fdisk -u gadget_drive
Device contains neither a valid DOS partition table, nor Sun, SGI
or OSF disklabel
Building a new DOS disklabel with disk identifier 0x6dd5552c.
Changes will remain in memory only, until you decide to write them.
After that, of course, the previous content won't be recoverable.

Warning: invalid flag 0x0000 of partition table 4 will be corrected by
w(rite)
You must set cylinders.
You can do this from the extra functions menu.

WARNING: DOS-compatible mode is deprecated. It's strongly recommended
to switch off the mode (command 'c').
```

```
Command (m for help): x
```

fdisk's -u option requests specifying a partition's starting and ending positions as sector numbers rather than cylinder numbers. Recent fdisk versions use sectors as the default.

gadget_drive is the name of the file created in step 1.

Enter s and the values below to create a 4-MB drive with 8 sectors/track, 1 head (1 track/cylinder), and 1024 cylinders. Each sector is 512 bytes, so the resulting "drive" has $512 \times 8 \times 1 \times 1024$, or 4,194,304, bytes.

```
Expert command (m for help): s
Number of sectors (1-63, default 63): 8
Warning: setting sector offset for DOS compatiblity

Expert command (m for help): h
Number of heads (1-256, default 255): 1

Expert command (m for help): c
Number of cylinders (1-1048576): 1024
```

Enter r to exit expert mode, and enter n to create and set up the emulated drive's primary partition 1, accepting the default sector numbers:

```
Expert command (m for help): r
Command (m for help): n
Command action
   e   extended
   p   primary partition (1-4)
p
Partition number (1-4): 1
First sector (8-8191, default 8): 8
Last sector, +sectors or +size{K,M,G} (8-8191, default 8191): 8191
```

Enter t and when prompted, enter the partition number and the code for the desired partition type. Type 83 is Linux:

```
Command (m for help): t
Selected partition 1
Hex code (type L to list codes): 83
```

Enter p to review the settings and w to save them:

```
Command (m for help): p

Disk gadget_drive: 4 MB, 4194304 bytes
```

```
1 heads, 8 sectors/track, 1024 cylinders, total 8192 sectors
Units = sectors of 1 * 512 = 512 bytes
Sector size (logical/physical): 512 bytes / 512 bytes
I/O size (minimum/optimal): 512 bytes / 512 bytes
Disk identifier: 0xd61275f0


Device Boot      Start         End      Blocks   Id  System
 gadget_drive        8        8191        4092   83  Linux


Command (m for help): w
The partition table has been altered!


Syncing disks.
```

3. Create a File System on the Emulated Drive

After creating the emulated drive, either the USB host or commands on the embedded system can create a file system on the emulated drive.

To let the USB host system create the file system, skip this step and use the instructions following step 5.

To create the file system when detached from the USB host, the embedded system must first associate a loop device with the drive's backing file. A loop device is a pseudo device that enables accessing a file as if it were a drive or other block device. This command uses the losetup command to associate the loop device at /dev/loop0 with a file named gadget_drive:

losetup -o 4096 /dev/loop0 gadget_drive

The -o option specified the byte offset of the partition in the emulated drive. In the fdisk example above, the first sector of the gadget_drive file's partition is sector 8. Thus the byte offset = 8 × 512, or 4096.

This command creates an ext3 file system on the loop0 loop device:

mkfs.ext3 /dev/loop0

If the emulated drive doesn't mount automatically, you can do so manually:

mkdir /media/gadget

mount /dev/loop0 /media/gadget

Device firmware can access the emulated drive, creating and modifying files and directories.

When firmware is finished accessing the drive, before attaching to a USB host, the system should unmount the drive and detach the file from the associated loop device:

```
umount /dev/loop0
losetup -d /dev/loop0
```

4. Assign the File as the Backing File

Before accessing the emulated drive from a USB host, the embedded system must load the g_file_storage module naming the backing file that will function as a drive. The modprobe command performs this function:

```
modprobe g_file_storage stall=0 file=gadget_drive
```

The stall parameter is optional, but setting stall=0 ensures that the device will return a STALL code only when no other legal option is available. The reason for this option is that some device controllers don't respond properly to the host's request to clear the HALT condition following a STALL.

5. Attach the Emulated Drive to a USB Host System

After enumeration, if the drive has a supported file system, the OS typically mounts the emulated drive, and host applications can read and write to files on the drive.

If necessary, you can mount the emulated drive manually, specifying the file system. On Linux systems, use the mount command with the -t option to specify a file system. The mount point (/media/5024-FF05 in this example) can be any existing directory:

```
mount -t ext3 /dev/sdb1 /media/5024-FF05
```

This command creates the file test1.txt on the emulated drive and stores a line of text in the file:

```
echo "Testing the gadget drive" >/media/5024-FF05/test1.txt
```

To find the mount point of a mounted drive, view or search /proc/mounts as described in Chapter 5.

The USB host expects exclusive access to the drive. Thus the embedded system shouldn't attempt to access a drive mounted by a USB host. For the same reason, when the embedded system has mounted the emulated drive, the USB host shouldn't attempt to access the drive.

Accessing the Emulated Drive on the Embedded System

To access the drive's files from the embedded system, with the OTG port detached from the USB host, associate a loop device with the backing file and mount the emulated drive as described in step 3:

```
losetup -o 4096 /dev/loop0 gadget_drive
mount /dev/loop0 /media/gadget
```

When the embedded system is finished accessing the drive, before reattaching to the host, unmount the emulated drive and detach it from the loop device:

```
umount /dev/loop0
losetup -d /dev/loop0
```

Let the Host Create the File System

If you don't create a file system for the backing file as described in step 3 above, the host system can perform the task.

On attaching the embedded system to a Linux host, look in the /dev directory on the host to find the emulated drive's device node.

Then use the mkfs command to create the file system specifying the emulated drive's device node.

Be sure you specify the device node for the emulated drive and not the device node for another system drive!

```
mkfs.ext3 /dev/sdb1
```

Using the OTG Port as a Host Port

On systems that use the BeagleBoard-xM's demo Ångström distribution, you can determine the port's current role by viewing the mode attributes of the musb_hdrc driver:

```
cd /sys/devices/platform/musb_hdrc
cat mode
```

The supported modes include:

b_idle   The port is functioning as a B-device and no host is attached.

b_peripheral The port is functioning as a B-device and a host is attached.

a_idle   The port is functioning as an A-device and no peripheral is attached.

a_host   The port is functioning as an A-device and a peripheral is attached.

On attaching a Micro-B plug, the port should function as a B-device. With no device attached, the mode should be b_idle. After configuring a system as a peripheral such as an emulated drive and attaching to a host, the mode should be b_peripheral, and the host should be able to access the emulated drive. On removing the attachment to the host, the mode should return to b_idle.

On attaching a Micro-A plug, the port should function as an A-device. With no device attached, the mode should be a_idle. On attaching a supported USB device, the mode should change to a_host, and the system should be able to access the device.

If the OS hasn't loaded the host driver, the port won't switch modes. Loading g_zero before attaching a device loads the host driver and enables the port to function as a host port:

```
modprobe g_zero
```

On a system that doesn't switch roles automatically, before using the port as a peripheral other than g_zero, you may need to do all of the following:

```
modprobe -r g_zero
losetup -o 4096 /dev/loop0 gadget_drive
umount /dev/loop0
modprobe g_file_storage stall=0 file=gadget_drive
```

modprobe -r removes the g_zero module, losetup associates a loop device with the emulated drive, umount unmounts the loop device if the OS has mounted it, and modprobe loads the module for the desired peripheral function:

Before using the port as a host port again, you may need to do the following:

```
modprobe -r g_file_storage
losetup -d gadget_drive
modprobe g_zero
```

modprobe -r unloads the module for the peripheral function, losetup removes the association with the loop device if present, and modprobe loads g_zero to enable functioning as a host port.

A patch that resolves the role-switching issue will be incorporated into future Ubuntu distributions with OTG support.

On systems using the Ångström distribution, this command enables the port to function as a host port:

```
echo host > /sys/devices/platform/musb_hdrc/mode
```

After executing this command, the port should switch roles automatically according to what is attached.

I hope you've found this book useful. To learn more about USB and embedded hosts, please visit my website at *janaxelson.com*. I wish you success with your projects!

Jan

Index

E

Eclipse IDE **29**

ECM (Ethernet control model) **85**

EEM (Ethernet emulation model) **85**

ehci_hcd **46**

electrical interface **17**

EMAC, Inc. **21, 22**

embedded PC
> USB host in **22**
> See also BeagleBoard-xM

embedded system **14**

endpoint
> defined **2**
> descriptor **11**

endpoint zero **5**

enumeration **4**

Epson Corporation **95, 98**

ESC/P language **95**

escape sequence **95**

Ethernet as alternative to USB drive **55**

Ethernet control model (ECM) **85**

Ethernet emulation model (EEM) **85**

ext3 file system **140, 141, 142**

F

FAT16 and FAT 32 **54**

fclose function **62, 65**

Feature report (HID) **68**

fgetc function **73**

file
> copying **31**
> reading **62–65**
> writing to **60–62**

file system
> in mass-storage device **54**
> root **25**

flash drive
> compatibility **54**
> See also mass storage

flush function **54**

Foomatic **100**

fopen function **62, 65**

form feed code **95**

fread function **65**

Freescale Semiconductor Inc. **21, 23, 25, 136**

FTDI **22**
> FT232x USB UART **5, 23**
> FT245x USB FIFO **79**
> USB virtual serial port chips **78**
> Vinculum II **23**

full speed
> defined **2**
> embedded hosts and **15**

Future Technology Devices International
> See FTDI

fwrite function **62**

G

gadget API **137–143**

gateway **87**

gcc. See toolchain

gdmsetup **31**

Generic Desktop control **68**

generic device driver **110**
> application **111–123**
> for HID **123–125**

GET_DEVICE_ID request **94**

Get_Status request (OTG) **136**

getch function **75**

GHI Electronics **22, 23–24**

Ghostscript **98**

gnome-bluetooth manager **91**

gnome-terminal **29**

GNU C library **29**

H

handshake phase (transaction) **2–3**

hardware, USB host **17–19**

hciconfig tool **90**

hcitool command **89–90**